AIR WAR NORMANDY

AIR WAR NORMANDY

by

RICHARD TOWNSHEND BICKERS

LEO COOPER

LONDON

First published in Great Britain in 1994 by
LEO COOPER
190 Shaftesbury Avenue, London WC2H 8JL
an imprint of
Pen & Sword Books Ltd
47 Church Street, Barnsley, South Yorkshire S70 2AS

ISBN 0 85052 412 1

A CIP catalogue record for this book is
available from the British Library

Typeset by CentraCet Limited, Cambridge
Printed in England by Redwood Books Ltd.
Trowbridge, Wilts.

ACKNOWLEDGMENTS

My thanks to the RAF Museum, the Imperial War Museum,
Service Historique de l'Armée de l'Air and Militârgeschtliches
Forschungsamt. Also to Lt-Col Victor Houart Belgian Air Force
Retd, and all others who kindly sent me their reminiscences.

CONTENTS

INTRODUCTION

Without air superiority the invasion of Normandy could not have succeeded, nor would the Allies have been able to follow it with the victorious campaign across France and the Low Countries that brought about Germany's unconditional surrender.

The first phase, from the landings to the break through the German front at Falaise six weeks later, was crucial to ultimate victory, Allied air superiority during that period prevented the *Luftwaffe* making any effective large-scale intrusion over the battle area. This gave the attacking naval and ground forces freedom of action during daylight hours, while the enemy was virtually immobilized because any movement provoked swift attack by fighter-bombers.

Aerial domination, not only over the beachhead and its immediate hinterland but also the whole of France – and even, with strong fighter escort, Germany – bestowed on Allied bombers the liberty to operate both strategically and tactically wherever and whenever either was needed. Thus, air superiority was as important in preventing the enemy's re-supply of his forces at the front, by bombing factories, as it was in covering the allied troops and airfields on the battlefield.

Although heavy bombers were essentially strategic weapons, they proved their tactical value on such occasions as the British and Canadian attack on Caen, when, as a preliminary, 450 Lancasters and Halifaxes softened the defences by dropping 2,500 tons of high explosive.

The specialist air force that fought in close co-operation with the armies was not created by any individual senior commander's sudden stroke of genius. It was the product of four years' development in other theatres of war, with its roots in the fighting in France during 1917 and 1918, when much was learned about air/land co-operation but neglected between then and 1940.

The Second Tactical Air Force, known as 2nd TAF, was formed specifically for the invasion of Normandy and the France and Germany Campaign that would ensue. It was so named because the first tactical air force already existed, but not under that title; it was Desert Air Force, born in the North African Campaign that began in 1940 and now operating in Italy. The necessity for close co-operation between the RAF and Eighth Army in the Western Desert had given it birth and nurtured its development, through which evolved the system of Air/Land liaison that was the basis of 2nd TAF's organization.

By October, 1942, two armies, each with its own air component, were fighting their way to Tunis, The British and Commonwealth Eighth Army, with RAF squadrons, advanced from the east, while a combined British and American force, with RAF and USAAF squadrons, approached to join it from the west. On 18 February, 1943, British Commonwealth and American squadrons were combined in a new formation, North-West African Tactical Air Force. It was commanded by Air Marshal Sir Arthur Coningham, hitherto commanding Desert Air Force – which now came under NWATAF and continued its task for Eighth Army across Sicily and up the length of Italy. This was the first use of the title Tactical Air Force.

Coningham, in his first directive, gave air supremacy as his command's prime purpose. This would enable land forces to operate practically without hindrance from the enemy air force and permit the RAF and USAAF increased freedom in the battle area and the enemy's rear. It was achieved. Addressing Parliament at the time of Operation Overlord, the Normandy landings, Winston Churchill, with his usual felicity of expression, described it as the combined employment of land, air and sea forces in the highest degree of intimacy.

That the close support system which had proved so successful was recreated in 2nd TAF was ensured by the choice of its leaders. Neither General Dwight Eisenhower, Supreme Allied Commander, nor Air Marshal Sir Traford Leigh-Mallory, Allied Air Commander-in-Chief for the coming invasion and campaign, had had direct involvement with DAF or NWATAF, but 2nd TAF's senior commanders had.

Air Chief Marshal Sir Arthur Tedder, appointed Deputy Supreme Allied Commander, had been C-in-C RAF Middle East, which included North Africa, for two years. He had learned the need to establish good relations with Army commanders and had won their respect. Coningham, who had done more than anyone to evolve the idea of a tactical air force, was 2nd TAF's Air Officer Commanding. Air Vice-Marshal Harry Broadhurst, who had succeeded him in command of DAF, was given command of 83 Group in 2nd TAF. AVM L. O. Brown, who had, when a group captain, been AOC 202 Group in the embryo Desert Air Force was commander of 84 Group. Many of the wing and squadron commanders had also served in North Africa.

Germany had had the prescience to send a strong *Luftwaffe* contingent to fight for the Facists against the Communists in the Spanish Civil War of 1936–1939. In consequence her air force developed the most efficient fighter formation – loose fours – while every other country continued to fly tight threes. German Generals had invented the *Blitzkrieg* technique of close air force/armoured attack. It is remarkable that they had not been first in the field with a tactical air force linked to the ground forces.

Even though the Germans did not think of it for themselves, they had every chance to copy it. In North Africa the *Luftwaffe* and *Afrika Korps* had suffered defeat by the RAF and Army's flexible yet closely bonded co-operation. They occupied front-row stalls in this theatre of war and must have formed an accurate appreciation of the script to which the actors were performing. In Italy, where the Cab Rank method of employing ground-attack fighters most efficiently was originated, they could not have failed to learn, in action and from overheard radio messages between ground and air, how this supreme provision of battlefield air support was achieved. Yet they never emulated it.

The term D-Day generally recalls the Normandy landings. There had in fact been two others – the invasions of Sicily and Italy. Both were made under intense fire from the shore, accurate bombing and strafing from the air, flak *and strong fighter defence*, all of which inflicted heavy casualties on the invading sea, land and air forces. Casualties would have been even worse if the Allies had not already achieved air superiority, although it was not yet overwhelming, as it was to be over Normandy.

These earlier invasions, however, were not preceded by a dithyrambic exhortation in the manner of General Eisenhower's Order of the Day in June, 1944; nor did the British Commanders resort to exclamation marks.

Supreme Headquarters Allied Expeditionary Force
Soldiers, Sailors and Airmen of the Allied
Expeditionary Force!

You are about to embark upon the Great Crusade, toward [sic] which we have striven these many months [thirty for the USA, forty-six for the British Commonwealth, France and the other European Allies]. The eyes of the world are upon you. The hopes and prayers of liberty-loving people everywhere march with you. In company with our brave Allies and brothers-in-arms on other Fronts, you will bring about the destruction of the German war machine, the elimination of Nazi tyranny over the oppressed people of Europe, and security for ourselves in a free world.

Your task will not be an easy one. Your enemy is well trained, well equipped and battle-hardened. He will fight savagely.

But this is the year 1944! Much has happened since the Nazi triumphs of 1940–41. The United Nations have inflicted upon the Germans great defeats, in open battle, man-to-man. Our air offensive has seriously reduced their strength in the air and on the ground. Our Home Fronts have given us an overwhelming superiority in weapons and munitions of war, and placed at our disposal great reserves of trained fighting men. The tide has turned! The free men of the world are marching together to Victory!

I have full confidence in your courage, devotion to duty and skill in battle. We will accept nothing less than full Victory!

Good luck! And let us all beseech the blessing of Almighty God upon this great and noble undertaking.

This was the first war in which airborne troops had gone into action, which imposed a further function on the Allied air forces. It was also the war that proved that, whereas paratroop drops and the air-lifting of supplies would continue to be essential in most military operations, gliders were a grave hazard and must be abandoned.

The notion of transporting soldiers by air originated when Napoleon Bonaparte, avid to invade England, began assembling ships at Boulogne. He examined the feasibility of sending 2,500 balloons, each carrying four men, across the Channel to take the coastal defences in the rear. The enterprise would, of course, have failed. Unfortunately it was abandoned, or Europe would have been rid of the bumptious little upstart ten years before Waterloo.

In the Great War the American General Mitchell had proposed flying infantrymen in British Handley Page 0/100 bombers (wingspan 100 ft) behind German lines and dropping them by parachute, but his Commander-in-Chief vetoed it. Italy was the first country to experiment with paratroops, in 1927, and by 1930 two battalions were being trained. In 1928 the USA did some trials, concluded that parachutists would be useful only in small numbers as saboteurs and abandoned the proceedings. The Russian and German Armies were the most dedicated to building a paratroop force. By 1936 the Russians were able to astound observers, including military attachés at Moscow embassies, by demonstrating a descent by 1,500 soldiers with weapons and kit. In the same year Hitler ordered an Army parachute school to be started and in 1937 exercises began in the use of gliders for carrying weapons and ammunition. It was Germany's breathtaking use of comparatively small groups of paratroops in April, 1940, against Denmark and Norway, and in May against Holland and Belgium, that forced Britain and other countries to add parachute and, later, gliderborne troops to their Battle Order.

The aeroplanes and gliders that air crews returning to base from bombing, reconnaissance, intruder and counter-measure sorties saw early on D-Day for the invasion of Normandy, 6 June, 1944, were in staggering numbers. The RAF had 460 aeroplanes and 1,050 Horsa (40 troops or eight tons of cargo) and 70 Hamilcar (29 troops or three tons) gliders. Five Dakota, four Albemarle, four Stirling and two Halifax squadrons carried the British Sixth Airborne Division. The USAAF strength was 900 aeroplanes and more than 100 Waco gliders that could each lift fifteen troops. As with the airborne landings in Sicily a year earlier and from the same causes – flak, strong wind and navigational errors – the gliders were widely scattered on landing. The airborne formations' consequent casualties and loss of gear were far beyond the planners' estimate. Nonetheless, the Generals were grateful for them.

This repetition of what had happened in Sicily made it clear, however, that the transportation of a huge force of parachute and gliderborne troops could never avoid being subjected to the vagaries of weather, poor navigation, anti-aircraft fire, possible fighter interception . . . and panic. The last was a dire weakness that would always assail some pilots of both the towing aircraft and the towed, who swerved off the line to avoid artillery or machine-gune fire or released the glider prematurely – or were guilty of both.

The air war that contributed with such versatility to the defeat of the Germans in Normandy saw the last use of gliders in battle. They have been replaced by helicopters, which can lift heavy guns and vehicles slung beneath them, carry large numbers of troops, and deposit them precisely wherever they are ordered. The time to dispense with paratroops has not yet come and perhaps never will.

★

Although they were not defined as such, preparations for the invasion of the French mainland really began on the day when the last members of the British Expeditionary Force were evacuated from there in June, 1940.

Thenceforth every operational sortie that the RAF flew made a direct or indirect contribution to the Normandy landings four years later: Coastal Command sinking submarines and surface vessels; Bomber Command destroying German industrial plants; Fighter Command shooting down German fighters escorting enemy bombers and those that attacked the RAF's raids; Transport Command carrying paratroops or towing gliders laden with soldiers, light vehicles and supplies into action or on training flights; all were doing damage to the enemy war machine that would ultimately be of indispensable advantage to the Allies when the final blow was struck. The large-scale air, naval and Commando attack on Dieppe in August, 1942, was a rehearsal for the great enterprise whose date had not yet been decided.

Another facet of this vast and complicated undertaking that is also brought to light is the fighting competence in which officers and men of RAF ground branches and trades were trained especially for Operation Overlord. The RAF Regiment is a fighting corps formed to defend airfields, as infantry and anti-aircraft artillery. Other ground crew, usually regarded mistakenly as non-combatant, also had to be ready to fight. In addition to servicing aircraft, operating mobile radar units and driving vehicles, they were armed with Sten guns or rifles and taught to defend themselves and the sites on which they worked.

Why and how all these activities affected every element of the final onslaught is explained in the following pages.

1

LONG-TERM PREPARATIONS

The most conspicuous use of air power in preparation for the assault was shown by the fighters, bombers and fighter-bombers that did such devastation in the weeks leading up to the landings. But before an invasion fleet could set sail confidently there were several impediments to be eliminated. Much of this was done far from the public eye and unpublicized by the press and radio.

The least evident work was done by Coastal Command, which, like Fighter and Bomber, flew specific sorties that were essential to the invasion plan. These began years before dummy tanks, vehicles, guns and shipping were positioned about Britain or officers and aircraftmen in ground branches and trades were trained to use soldiers' weapons.

In 1940 the *Luftwaffe* had outnumbered the RAF. Its Me109s owned various advantages, besides numbers, over the Hurricanes that constituted two-thirds of the defending fighter force. They were almost the equal of the Spitfires in some respects and more heavily armed. Yet it was the outnumbered British fighters and the anti-aircraft batteries – whose gunners suffered more from enemy attacks than is usually acknowledged – that won the Battle of Britain.

Victory in the battle did not signal only the failure of the German Air Force to knock out the Royal Air Force, but also caused the cancellation of Hitler's plan to invade England in the summer of 1940. Frustration of that intention was owed, as many senior and highly decorated Battle of Britain pilots have pointed out, largely to Bomber Command's constant battering of the ports in which invasion barges were being assembled.

Bombing of cities by both sides did not break civilian morale, and when industry in Germany, Occupied France or Great Britain was the target, repairs were usually made more quickly than the other side expected. Neither superiority of numbers in the air in 1940 nor subsequent heavy bombing raids brought Britain to defeat. The U-boats, however, drove the country to the brink of starvation.

On the first day of the war U-boats began to sink British ships. In June, 1940, the month before the Battle of Britain began, they sank fifty-eight ships totalling 284,000 tons. For several months thereafter the average was 250,000 tons. The Royal Navy and RAF were sinking an increasing number of U-boats, but production of these exceeded losses. The German Focke-Wulf Condors, four-engined aeroplanes with a 2,206-mile range, 4,626lb bomb load and two cannons and six machine guns, were also preying on Allied ships. When Churchill, Roosevelt and Stalin met at Casablanca in January, 1943, to confer on strategy, they agreed that until the German submarine fleet was overcome an effective invasion of Europe was not practical.

The U-boats' richest hunting ground was the South-Western Approaches, through which convoys to and from England passed. The RAF's most rewarding area of action was the Bay of Biscay, which the German submarines had to cross when leaving their French ports for the Atlantic and on return. In 1944 No 19 Group was patrolling the Bay in great strength. There were six Wellington Squadrons, six of B24 Liberators, four of Sunderlands, two of Halifaxes and one of Mosquitoes. Three Beaufighter squadrons patrolled off the French coast to protect the U-boat hunters from Me109s and 110s, Fw190s and Ju88s. The Group also operated four Fleet Air Arm squadrons: two Swordfish, two TBF Avenger and four US Navy B24 squadrons.

As with the scarcely acknowledged contribution of Bomber Command to the deliverance that victory in the Battle of Britain bestowed, so the stupendous effort of Coastal Command in its anti-submarine operations was a generally unappreciated yet essential factor in the success of Overlord. The diligent and arduous patrols of eight and a half to eighteen hours – depending on the type of aircraft – went on day and night, behind the scenes and hundreds of miles from Normandy.

This duty demanded intense concentration by the whole crew and entailed its own characteristic dangers. In order for the airborne radar (ASV – air to surface vessel) to operate at its best, crews were briefed to fly at 500ft, or, if fitted with a radio altimeter, 450ft. If an engine failed at that height, there was barely enough time for the pilot of a twin-engine type such as a Wellington (Hudsons were no longer on operations) to take remedial action before hitting the sea. Many captains flew at a prudent 750ft. There was always the threat of enemy air attack. One aircraft, even a Liberator with its eight .50 machine guns or Sunderland, which had eight .303 and two .50, was at a disadvantage against Ju88 long-range fighters attacking by daylight in pairs or fours. By day a U-boat on the surface would most often fight back with cannon and machine guns. At night, when the ASV picked up a surfaced submarine and the aircraft switched on its powerful Leigh Light (a 24-inch searchlight) preparatory to a bombing or depth charge run, the vessel usually gave battle with 20mm flak.

The war had been going on for two years before a Coastal Command success dramatic enough to compare with the spectacular achievements of Fighter and Bomber Commands was released to the press and BBC. It was an arresting feat in itself and made all the more remarkable because it was performed before the introduction of ASV and by the least well equipped of all the Coastal types – a Hudson. This rather humble aeroplane was originally an airliner, the Lockheed 14 Super Electra. The RAF variant was fitted with twin fixed machine guns firing forward, a ventral gun that had to be lowered before firing and a two-gun turret above the fuselage, well aft and covering the rear. Its bomb load was 1,000lb, endurance seven hours and it carried no radar.

★

James Thompson had sold cars and lorries before the war. Now he was a squadron leader in 269 Squadron and pilot of a MkVI Hudson. The others in the crew were the second pilot/navigator, wireless operator and rear gunner. Frequent rain squalls obscured the visibility and whipped the sea to whitecaps. They had been on patrol for a couple of hours when the navigator, in the nose, reported a U-boat on the surface 1,000 yards on the port bow. The pilot immediately dived towards it and as the Hudson crossed it diagonally from the starboard quarter the navigator released the bombs, which hurled up waterspouts close to the target. While the Hudson turned, the rear gunner reported that the submarine was still above water on an even keel. The wireless operator lowered the belly gun. The navigator was at the front guns and both men opened fire. When the aircraft had recrossed the U-boat the rear gunner took up the shooting.

The Hudson's crew had expected the U-boat to dive, but instead the conning tower hatch opened and German sailors began clambering out. The airmen thought they were about to man the U-boat's gun, so continued firing. The men on deck turned back to retreat into the conning tower, while more of their comrades were emerging. Men were falling all over the deck, some under the aircraft's bullets, others through collision. By the time Thompson had made four runs over the submarine someone aboard had found a white shirt to wave in surrender.

Thompson ordered his crew to stop firing, then circled their victim while his wireless operator signalled their base and Group Headquarters. For the next three and a half hours they patrolled round the U-boat in the turgid light and continuing heavy rain showers and gusting wind. A Catalina flying boat, whose endurance was 17½ hours, relieved them. To impress on its captain that the U-boat had surrendered and ensure that he would not attack it, Thompson told his WOP to signal, 'Look after our, repeat our, submarine, which showed the white flag'. The answer was brief: 'O.K.' Before quitting the scene, Thompson made a low pass over his U-boat and some of its crew waved a farewell.

Command and Group Headquarters suspected that the submarine's commander might try to make a crash dive in the worsening weather when daylight waned. Other Coastal aircraft in the area were ordered to share the vigil, doubling up with the Catalina, which stayed at its post for eight hours. Before nightfall a destroyer arrived on the scene and exchanged lamp signals with the U-boat. During the night the wind strengthened to gale force and when another Catalina turned up at first light it was repeatedly blown off course. Each time it took ten to twenty minutes to find the submarine again, guided by the light that she had been ordered to show. As the morning lengthened corvettes arrived to keep watch, with a relay of attendant Catalinas. From the time when the destroyer joined the first Catalina, aircraft were in position by day and night for forty hours. The Hudson's Captain and navigator won the DFC for this exploit; the wireless operator and air gunner were, as often happened to Other Ranks, given no award.

There was a widespread supposition that Coastal Command crews must have a phlegmatic dispoition to endure long, tedious hours spent on successive sorties that yielded no contact with the enemy to relieve the monotony of visually searching hundreds of square miles of grey sea. There was an implication of stolid men with unimaginative minds fitted to a task that would drive a fighter pilot into a state of frantic boredom because he could not throw a few aerobatics, and give bomber crews a feeling of guilt because they weren't being shot at all the time by flak and having bombs whistling past dropped by chums flying above. In truth, Coastal crews' wits were no slower nor their sense of humour any less macabre than the rest of the RAF's.

A fighter pilot might content himself, discussing a friend's recent fatal dive into the ground and being asked, 'What was he doing?' with the seemingly callous reply, 'About six hundred knots'. A Coastal pilot might not be so slick, but would show the same traditional RAF irreverence for calamity.

There was an occasion during the pre-invasion period when a Wellington spotted three lifeboats adrift. They were some 300 miles offshore and loaded with survivors from a torpedoed warship. Having signalled the find to base and received an answer that naval vessels were on their way, the Wellington's captain told his wireless operator to make the following lamp signal: 'To the bell-bottomed nautics from us. A destroyer of the Royal Navy is on her way and should arrive in twelve hours. A Catalina will probably come and say good day too. Just think of the people who pay thousands to go sailing. Good luck.'

In the most critical and busiest pre-Normandy months, U-boats hunted in large packs and their manufacture was at its zenith. In a running fight, a Liberator navigator, Flying Officer Layton, earned a DSO and his pilot, Squadron Leader Bulloch, who already had this decoration, a bar to it. They were patrolling in company with another Liberator over a convoy bound from the USA to Britain that was involved in thirty-five U-boat attacks in four days. Bulloch had been on patrol less than half an hour, in a hailstorm, when his crew sighted a U-boat. It was on the surface, ten miles astern of the convoy but catching up. It spotted the Liberator and crash-dived, but Bulloch arrived over the swirls it had created before they subsided, so had a good aiming mark. He dropped a stick of six depth charges. After the geysers and spume and general turbulence created by the explosions had settled, a third of the U-boat's length was protruding above the sea at a thirty-degree angle, oil formed a half-mile slick and flotsam was tossed about by the waves. One of the escorting warships signalled: 'You killed him.' Another, 'You certainly got him.' The third was more specific: 'Dead bodies seen.'

Within three hours Bulloch sighted two more U-boats that were 300 yards apart and overhauling their prey. He dropped his remaining six depth charges across the nearer one and saw a huge waterspout result before he resumed his hunt.

Being posted to a Sunderland, Catalina or Coastal Liberator squadron was regarded as a privilege, for these behemoths among aeroplanes and flying boats offered a comparatively comfortable existence on duty. Because of their long patrols, they were equipped with rest bunks and, a much envied perquisite, a galley in which hot meals were cooked. The standard fare was steak and potatoes, followed, of course by pudding. Bulloch had switched in the automatic pilot (universally known to civilian and Service pilots as George) and was balancing his plate on his lap when another U-boat came in sight. He switched George out and sounded the alarm. His lunch slipped to the cockpit floor as he dived the Liberator on the enemy, machine guns and cannon firing. Shell and bullet strikes ensured that the U-boat slid below the surface, where its speed was reduced by two-thirds. Holes in the conning tower and hull must have forced it to return to base at once.

One year before the Normandy D-Day, Air Chief Marshal Sir Charles Portal (later Marshal of the RAF Lord Portal), Chief of the Air Staff, sent this message to the AOC-in-C Coastal Command, Air Marshal Sir John Slessor. 'I wish to express to you and all under your command my admiration and warmest thanks for your achievements in the anti-U-boat war in the month just ended. The brilliant success achieved in this vital field is the well-deserved result of tireless perseverance and devotion to duty, and is, I am sure, a welcome reward for the air crews and others who have spared no effort during long months of arduous operations and training. Now that you have obtained this remarkable advantage over the U-boat I know you will press it home with ever-increasing vigour and determination, until, in conjunction with the Royal Navy, you have finally broken the enemy's morale.'

By one month before D-Day 807 of the 1150 U-boats launched had been sunk and eighty-five per cent of their crews were dead or prisoners. Without Coastal Command's share in this, the men and weapons for the landings could not have been assembled in Britain, nor could the invasion fleet have crossed the Channel without crippling losses. But few people have ever known that or would associate maritime air operations in the Western Approaches and the Bay of Biscay with the Normandy beachheads.

An armada of slow ships crossing the English Channel was the juiciest of targets for enemy submarines. Ten or twenty of them could have played merry hell with the invasion vessels. On D-Day thirty-five U-boats were at the German High Command's disposal to operate in the area and on 6 June sixteen of these were detailed to sail for the Channel. Between that day and 10 June Coastal Command sank six. Thanks to Ultra, the apparatus that could break any German code, the enemy's intentions were known to the RAF and Royal Navy. The Germans sent no more U-boats to the Channel unless they were one of the few fitted with *Schnorkel*, the breathing equipment that enabled them to charge their batteries without surfacing. Soon they were sending none at all.

The long-term planning that culminated in an invasion carried out without hindrance in the air or under the waters of the English Channel called for no more important or unpublicized activity than Coastal Command's. Its connection with the storming of the Normandy beaches remains as unappreciated by the other Services and RAF Commands as it was then.

While Coastal Command was subduing the German undersea fleet, Bomber Command and the USAAF day bombers concentrated on targets in Germany whose destruction or damage would reduce the German Air Force's and Army's ability to repulse the invasion or delay the Allies' advance to Berlin. The *Luftwaffe* felt the effects of strategic bombing months before D-Day.

The consequences would have been even more dire if the synthetic oil plants had been attacked two years before. It was what the German High Command feared above all, yet the Allies did not give them the highest priority until 8 June, 1944. Hydrogenation plants producing aviation petrol were the most strongly defended – surrounded by flak and barrage balloons, camouflaged and hidden by smoke screens. The fighter force was told to attack in strength any bomber formation that headed towards them. Decoy plants were built.

The first mass raids specifically planned in preparation for the invasion were made by 935 US 8th Air Force heavy bombers on

12 May, 1944, against fuel plants in central and eastern Germany. A new era had begun that Albert Speer, the Armaments Minister, warned Hitler would mean the end of armament production. He also told him, 'The enemy has struck us at one of our weakest points. If they persist at it this time, we will soon no longer have any fuel production worth mentioning. Our one hope is that the other side has an Air Force General Staff as *zerstreut liegend* [scatterbrained] as ours.'

It took only two weeks to put the plants back in production, but they were attacked again two days later, at the same time as others, as well as the Ploesti refinery in Romania, whose output was halved. A large part of the available RAF and USAAF bombers was employed in support of the invasion and by 22 June production of synthetic fuel had been reduced to ten per cent of normal. Three months later it was only five and a half per cent. Not only were aircraft, tanks and motor vehicles deprived of petrol, but the same plants also made nitrogen and methanol, which were necessary for the manufacture of explosives.

Nonetheless, deeply damaging though strategic bombing was, it could not win the war. No form of air operations can do that. It is the infantryman, with rifle, bayonet and grenades, who has to take and hold ground. Ahead of him, however, goes the armour. They must all be accompanied by another use of aircraft – tactical air support.

Right up until H-Hour on D-Day, day and night, the four-engined bombers were still pounding the enemy's West Wall of reinforced concrete and coastal artillery. The experience of one senior American pilot on the eve of D-Day is indicative of the ferocity of the defences in what the Germans knew must be the last hours before the awaited onslaught. Lieutenant-Colonel Leon Vane was co-pilot in a B17 leading a raid whose target lay near Wimereux. During the bombing run, flak hit the aircraft several times, killed the pilot, wounded Vane so severely that it almost severed his right foot and knocked out three engines. He kept the aircraft in position at the head of the formation. When he turned for base, the wireless operator put a tourniquet on his foot. To maintain flying speed he had to put the B17 into a shallow dive that he hoped would take it across the Channel.

There was an unexploded bomb aboard, so when he reached the English coast he told his crew to bale out. From what he heard on the intercom, he understood that one wounded man was unable to do so. To save the man's life, he decided to ditch, which would allow some chance of being picked up by a RAF air/sea rescue boat before they both drowned. His partly severed foot was trapped under his seat, so he was unable to use rudder and had to manoeuvre with ailerons and elevators. He set the aeroplane down on the water, his foot still jammed. As the aircraft was sinking an explosion blew him into the sea where he clung to wreckage while he inflated his life jacket. Then he began to look for the other survivor but could not find him. He was picked up a quarter of an hour later by Air Sea Rescue. In hospital, he learned that the man whom he thought had been left behind when the rest of the crew jumped had actually been able to get out with them. Vane was awarded the Congressional Medal of Honour, the USA's highest decoration.

The dialectic of pure logic does not apply to meteorology and probably never will. In the mid-twentieth century, without satellites and other refinements, it was often disastrously inaccurate. One airman who made a valuable contribution to the verification of weather forecasts, which enabled the USAAF heavy bombers to avoid having to abort their missions when storms or dense cloud unexpectedly barred their way was Colonel Budd Peaslee. His ingenuity ensured that they could maintain the essential unceasing pre-invasion bombardment.

When America took up arms Peaslee was, at forty-three, considered too old to fly fighters; but come invasion time and there he was in the cockpit of a Mustang. He and the eight other bomber pilots who had completed a tour of operations and volunteered to join him were known as air scouts. An image of bare knees and wide-brimmed hats comes to mind: they would have been better called weather reconnaissance pathfinders.

Whatever the name, their function was an intelligent and indispensable concept. It arose from Peaslee's remembered frustration on many sorties when he had arrived over a target and found it hidden by cloud. He expounded his bright idea to his Division Commander, whose response was that it sounded workable and was badly needed. He referred Peaslee to General Doolittle, Commander of the 8th Air Force, who told him to explain his plan to the two other Division Commanders. Having got their approval, Peaslee reported back to Doolittle, who authorized its acceptance. Thus First Scouting Force came into being, with the radio code name Buckeye Red.

Its task was to reconnoitre ahead of the bombers and report weather over the target. The first time the innovation was tried Munich was the target and the forecast was of excellent weather over Europe. Peaslee took off twenty minutes after the bombers. With the fighter's greater speed, he reached Munich twenty minutes before the Flying Fortresses were due, noted where the clouds were massed, flew back and met the bombers. At their briefing the pilots had been told to turn right after bombing. Peaslee called the formation leader and told him he should turn left. The division in which Peaslee's small unit served lost no aircraft that day. The other divisions, operating without air scouts, lost nine. Thenceforth they formed their own scouting forces. Lives were lost among the weather reconnaissance pilots, but bombing accuracy improved and fewer operations had to be abandoned. They also informed the RAF air/sea rescue service about the position of crews who had ditched, reported the take-off of enemy fighters and led damaged bombers home.

A B17 co-pilot with a distinction that was improbably different from the act that won Vane a decoration was an Englishman. Flight Lieutenant Jeffries was an RAF survivor of the the First World War who rejoined for the Second. No awards came his way – campaign medals only. Nobody knew his first name – he was 'Jeff' to everyone, from the Air Officer Commanding to the most junior pilot officer. He contrived to get himself attached to the USAAF for a while.

Having done his share on D-Day by some arcane wangling of the kind known only to veterans in any profession, he found himself in Italy towards the end of the war, still hanging on to flying duties, mostly testing aircraft after repair at maintenance units. Usually genial, he was in a fractious mood at the officers' mess bar one evening. A young colleague asked him what was the matter. Jeff produced a photograph of himself in the co-pilot's seat of a B17 with the aircraft's captain beside him. It was inscribed 'To Jeff, the best co-pilot I ever flew with.'

'That's a nice line, Jeff. So, what are you binding about?' his friend asked.

'They won't let me fly Spitfires – they think I'll black out,' Jeff complained. Pause for a laugh that sounded strangely like a giggle. 'They don't know I already black out in Hurricanes.'

Flight Lieutenant Jeffries was fifty-three years old.

He was not, however, the oldest pilot to fly a fighter. That honour must go – disturbingly, one supposes, for those whom he led – to an Italian. When Italy surrendered in September, 1943, some Italian Air Force squadrons elected to operate against the Germans. They were given the status of co-belligerents, not allies. The commanding officer of one Macchi squadron was seventy-three.

2

DECEPTION

Reconnaissance and deception were the central stratagems in preparation for a second invasion of Europe. Detailed planning began after the Dieppe raid by air, sea and land on 19 August, 1942. The first invasion of the European mainland was made in Italy on 3 September, 1943. Both operations taught the Allies much from which to profit when the time came to launch the ultimate assault. This must not merely succeed, but be overwhelming and lead to swift local victory followed by a short, fast-moving campaign that would end the war in Europe.

The plans for Overlord were masked by the most elaborate deceptions in the history of warfare, the most ingenious since the Greeks tricked their way into Troy with the mythical wooden horse.

Deception had two purposes: to conceal Allied activity from the enemy and to mislead him about the area to be invaded. Although the Allies had air superiority, it was impossible to prevent German reconnaissance aircraft and spies obtaining some information. Misdirection became the key. The enemy could and would learn that the invasion he expected from the moment when the USA entered the war was imminent. Therefore it was essential for its planners to delude him about where it would be aimed.

Great numbers of landing ships and smaller craft were being assembled while canvas dummies were moored in the tidal creeks on the Essex and Suffolk coasts. Collapsible plywood gliders were set up on bogus airfields in Kent and Sussex.

13

Inflatable tanks and artillery pieces were placed in south-east England. Dummy pumping stations were built on the Sussex coast to suggest that they were terminals for fuel lines that would supply vehicles embarking, and motor gunboats and torpedo boats sailing to strike at the Pas de Calais.

One of the most remarkable inventions for Overlord was the offshore harbour codenamed Mulberry. It was made of hollow concrete blocks, 230ft long, 60ft wide and 60ft deep, that were to be towed to the operational area, where they would be put together. There was no way to protect them from enemy photographic reconnaissance or the eyes of the local populace, so they were openly described as boom defences for British ports.

There were more than seventy radar stations between Dunkirk and St Malo. They could not all be bombed out of action, so had to be deceived by false signals traffic and messages in fictitious codes, but without blocking the Allies' channels of radio communication with one another or with the Resistance organizations in the occupied European countries. The BBC took part in these measures.

Field Marshal Montgomery's double, Captain Maurice Edward Clifton James of the Army Pay Corps, appropriately dressed, was driven daily for some weeks to a mythical Head-quarters on North Foreland. Shortly before D-Day he was flown to Gibraltar. The enemy, informed by spies in Algeciras, across the bay, who kept watch through binoculars, concluded that no invasion could be imminent if Monty were abroad; it also added credence to the theory that the south of France would prove to be the invasion site. The latter proved partly right, but when the Allies landed there two months after Normandy, it was against such light opposition that they suffered only 183 casualties.

The British public were asked to send hoarded picture post-cards and holiday snapshots of the French coast to the War Office. The British Embassies in selected neutral countries, Sweden, Switzerland, Spain and Portugal, made overt search for copies of Michelin map sheet 441, which covered the Pas de Calais.

The whole complicated business was reminiscent of a surrealist painting, turning around on itself and inverting in whorls and sequences that bemused the observers. Despite these widespread convolutions, involving thousands of participants, security was effectively maintained.

One of the warnings given by the disaster at Dieppe on 19 August, 1942, was that the admonition 'Careless Talk Costs Lives', familiar on posters everywhere since the beginning of the war, was no mere slogan. The raiding force had comprised 6,100 troops, 237 small ships among which were eight destroyers, forty-five RAF and three USAAF Spitfire squadrons, eight Hurricane, three Typhoon, five Boston, two Blenheim, four Mustang, one Beaufighter RAF squadron and four USAAF B17 squadrons. The enemy was not taken by surprise. Now, with nearly three million men under the orders of the Supreme Commander, General Eisenhower, and civilian scientists, codebreakers and numerous other specialists also involved, to maintain secrecy would verge on the miraculous. But it was done.

One means of keeping the Germans guessing was to position the shipping to be used in the invasion around the English, Scottish and Welsh coasts. One of Hitler's intuitions was that Norway would be the target for either the main or a diversionary landing. The presence of ships in north-eastern harbours encouraged this notion. But all these vessels would have to start moving south in the last week of May, an indication that the attack would be made somewhere between Brest and Ostend. A study of this coastline and the Atlantic Wall defences that the Todt Organization had built, using enforced French labour as well as German, would reveal to the German General Staff that the most favourable stretch was from Le Havre to Cherbourg. They would assume that the Allies had made the same evaluation. Still, there was also the caveat that the devious planners would probably not take the obvious route, but would go instead for the shortest crossing. Hence all the misleading activity in the south-east of England while the real preparations were going on two hundred miles west.

About the dummies used in deception there were esoteric

details that make one appreciate the intricacies of the lure-makers' craft.

In the First World War arifield camouflage had reached a level of expertise that baffled aircraft cameras and the human eye. In the Second World War anyone creeping up on dummy aircraft, tanks, guns or lorries and scrutinizing them through binoculars could spot the sham. But this, in the minds of those who fought their war in this manner, immediately suggested another double bluff – misdirection, as used by stage illusionists. Would real tanks, artillery and soft-skinned vehicles replace these dummies after spies, having seen the artificial ones, had sent messages to Germany?

There was a distinction between strategic and tactical dummies. The strategic sort were made of steel tubing or timber and covered with plywood or canvas; the tactical variety had to be easily transportable and swiftly erected. By the time that preparations for D-Day got under way, a year in advance, there was a gallimaufry of choices. On offer were towable or self-driving tanks and other vehicles; collapsible wood and canvas ones that were supported by guy ropes; painted mats that simulated foxholes or trenches. Some individual items were available in a variety of forms, such as the Sherman tank, which came either mobile, inflatable or folding.

The technicalities in the domain of materials were equally esoteric. The essential characteristics of a dummy were that it must be a convincing copy of the real item, easily transportable, quick to set up and keep its shape. The American high-pressure inflatable dummies were considered the best, because they were made of thinner rubber than their British counterparts, could be blown up to a greater degree of hardness and were less vulnerable to punctures. In the field, however, even the most artistic and workmanlike artefacts were destructible by both direct and indirect enemy action. Whereas a canvas and wood item would be blown to smithereens only by direct hits, the *de luxe* model in thin rubber could be holed by bomb and shell fragments from explosions a hundred yards away, as well as by bullets or by stones scattered far and wide by high explosive.

The inventive genius of those who were engaged on this research also came up with sonic equipment in the form of wire recorders – these worked on the same principle as modern tape recorders – that reproduced battle noises: the clatter of tanks, the thuds and detonations of artillery fire, the chatter of machine guns, the single shots of rifles, the sounds made by lorries and tanks, even the distinctive sounds of troops storming ashore, shouted orders and cries of the wounded.

The RAF and USAAF had dropped dummy parachutists in North Africa and Sicily that were equipped with a device which would prevent the enemy detecting that they were a deception. This was an explosive charge that destroyed the rubber figure by setting it on fire, which suggested that the man had burned his parachute and lay hidden, ready for action or sabotage. (But wasn't there a smell of burning rubber, to spoil the delusion?)

At the same time, by various complicated methods, including the use of double agents to misinform the Germans, Hitler and his Staff were persuaded that, if a landing were made in Normandy, it would be a mere feint to draw the bulk of the German forces away from the Pas de Calais, which was the true invasion site.

3

AIRCRAFT SIMULATE AN INVASION FLEET

On the night preceding D-Day, one of the most skilful operations of the war was entrusted to 617 Squadron, the renowned Dam Busters, now commanded by Wing Commander Leonard Cheshire, VC DSO and two bars, DFC. Five weeks beforehand, the Air Officer Commanding 5 Group, Air Vice-Marshal the Hon Ralph Cochrane AFC (later Air Chief Marshal, knighted and made GBE KCB) told Cheshire that his squadron would be doing no operations for the next month, while training for a very special one.

'Everyone must know that we'll have to invade France very soon,' said Cochrane. 'If the weather's favourable, it'll be in about a month's time. The landings will be west of Le Havre and we must trick Jerry into thinking they'll be somewhere else.'

There was not much scope for any original comment in reply. 'Well, I never!' hardly seemed to fit the case. Nor would 'Oh, right', as people say today, like robots – the inane response that serves to acknowledge every statement from 'I've mislaid my handkerchief' to 'I've got to have both legs amputated tomorrow.'

To be entrusted with Top Secret information that had, presumably, been witheld even from officers greatly senior to oneself made the mind reel. No 617's Commanding Officer let it pass in silence, probably thinking, '*Now*, what abnormal task have they got up their sleeves for us?'

'On the night before the landings,' Cochrane went on, 'a convoy fourteen miles wide will cross the Channel.'

'I suppose it'll have to be at least that size, sir, if the invasion's going to succeed.'

'That won't be the invasion: a dummy convoy will head for Cap d'Antifer, on the other side of Le Havre from the real invasion area.'

'I didn't know we'd got enough ships to put on an invasion *and* a spoof.'

'We haven't. The bluff is going to be done by your chaps.'

Radar could give early warning of an approaching fleet and there was only one way of misleading it, strips of metal foil, dropped by bombers, which looked exactly like aircraft echoes on a radar screen and were used to confuse the enemy defences during raids on Germany. The British thought they had invented it in 1942, but the assumption that the enemy would soon copy it delayed its use until 24 July, 1943, when 728 aircraft bombed Hamburg. The Germans had, in fact, already invented the device for themselves – they called it *Duppel* – and refrained from using it for the same reason. Its RAF codename was Window and this was the word that Cheshire exclaimed now.

'Yes, and it's going to mean the most accurate flying you've ever done.'

All the calculations to create the illusion of a large number of ships travelling at seven knots had been made. The aircraft dropping Window would have to fly at 3,000ft in formation, two miles apart and therefore invisible to one another, and do a lot of intricate manoeuvring while keeping within twenty feet of their required height and three seconds of their time at each turning point.

The task would take several hours and need two formations, each of eight aircraft, one seven miles astern of the other.

Each aircraft would fly for thirty-five seconds at 200 mph on a course parallel to the French coast, make a slow 180-degree turn, fly on the new heading for thirty-two seconds, then turn again onto the new reciprocal, throwing out Window at precise intervals also measured in seconds. Each initial course would be slightly ahead of where the previous one had started and the first bundle of Window dropped on it must coincide with the moment when the first bundle dropped on the preceding leg landed on the sea. In this way there would be an unbroken succession of returns on the enemy's cathode ray tubes. Each wave would keep this up for eight hours.

Cheshire's comment was that his crews were good enough to do all that was required of them, but were not going to be happy 'doing a stooge job on invasion night'.

'There'll be no flying task more important than this on invasion night,' Cochrane assured him. 'Tell them that. The fact that they might not be fired at is beside the point.'

Suppressing pilots' and flying crews' eagerness to get to grips with the enemy, whether they were in a fighter, bomber or any other type of squadron, meant that they had to find some other outlet for their fizzing high spirits, energy and the hidden desperation of knowing that the odds on surviving an operational tour were against them. It manifested itself in numerous strange ways. Several officers at Coningsby, where 617 was stationed, kept dogs that made free of the mess. One, a Scottie, had an infuriating habit of ambushing people as they passed a doorway, darting out and biting their ankles. Imitating its eccentric behaviour became a popular prank. A certain flight lieutenant, seeing a friend about to climb the stairs one evening, hid in a dark corner, on hands and knees, ready to spring. Footsteps approached. He pounced, bit, heard a grunt of astonishment and pain, and looked up. He found himself gazing at a total stranger who happened to be spending the night in the mess – a wing commander at that.

Cheshire's restless intelligence suggested that, as the Germans would be equally expecting an invasion, they might pre-empt it by dropping paratroops on British airfields. He therefore suggested that as many aircrew as possible should be provided with a rifle, Sten gun or hand grenade in addition to the revolver that was standard issue. It was not this usually wise young officer's happiest idea.

Ebullient young men who were accustomed to living on their nerves and, when bad weather caused operations to be cancelled, celebrated the reprieve from several hours of discomfort and danger by riotous behaviour in their messes, were bored by their present daily grind of total concentration for long periods on an arduous rehearsal. They greeted the issue of firearms like mischievous boys let loose with Roman candles, squibs and firecrackers. The officers set up plates on the lawn and fired Sten guns at them from windows. They lobbed grenades towards the Sergeants' Mess. One of them amused himself by sitting at his bedroom window at night and firing Sten bursts over the heads of late-returning comrades, who had to drop prone and crawl across the lawn. After three days Cheshire ordered all weapons to be returned to the armoury. Deprived of their toys, two frustrated pilots climbed onto the roof and dropped a Verey cartridge down a chimney from which smoke was emerging. They thought it was the Adjutant's (a flight lieutenant) and should have known better: only squadron leaders and above had a suite that comprised a sitting-room with a grate. It happened to be Cheshire's in which a fire was burning. The explosion brought him racing out of the building. He spotted the two miscreants on the roof, but kept silent. They, however, found themselves jointly Orderly Officers for a week.

Besides 617's Lancasters, a Stirling squadron, No 218, rehearsed a similar flying pattern, known as a creeping line ahead, while dropping window. Concurrently, on the night of D-minus-one, two fleets of small craft would set to sea from Newhaven and cruise at seven knots towards France, towing barrage balloons that floated above them at a carefully calculated height. These had radar reflectors that gave responses on the receivers' screens similar to those made by 10,000-ton ships.

Before the heavy bombers left their patrol lines and returned to base, they saw aeroplanes towing gliders streaming towards Normandy to deliver the right hook for which their straight left feint had made the enemy partly drop his guard.

4

D-MINUS-ONE ·

A n hour or so before midnight on 5 June three Albemarles took off from Brize Norton and three from Harwell, carrying engineer paratroops. Squadron Leader Leonard Archer (Later Wing Commander DSO OBE AFC), a flight commander in 296 Squadron, stationed at Brize Norton, was airborne at 2300. His passengers' task was to blow up gun emplacements in Normandy and set up a flarepath that would guide the glider-towing aircraft, due soon after, to their landing ground. To be selected for this operation was a testimonial to an air crew's efficiency. Faultless navigation was the criterion: the gliderborne force had to be concentrated in the right place.

The squadrons had carried out trials to determine the best crews. Leonard Archer says, 'We flew long distances out to sea, returning to photograph at night an obscure crossroads in Dorset. On D night we were pathfinders – a tribute to our magnificent navigator. We did not realize the significance – we were to be the first flights from this country in the battle to liberate Europe.'

Flying on any sort of operation in an Albemarle was one of the least attractive duties. Although designed as a bomber, this type was never used as such and entered squadron service in January, 1943, as a glider tug and special transport for the airborne forces. It was slow and poorly armed, its only defence twin Vickers hand-operated K guns mounted amidships.

'Weather was good. We approached the French coast in a dark overcast sky, hoping we could see enough features to pinpoint our position. All the crew knew the route by heart: up to 5,000ft over coastal light flak, skirt the canal, cross it to the north, over Ouistreham, reduce height to 1,000ft, 140 knots (God, we're loitering), pick up the small lake, prepare to jump.

'Navigator to get us to the dropping zone, the gunner vigilant for opposition, wireless op helping the departing guests, and the pilot obeying orders for height, speed, direction.

'On track and our DZ [dropping zone] identified ahead. All is quiet and we warn the passengers. No time or inclination for words like "good luck" – we said it all before. Now the intercom will take only necessities: height 600ft . . ."left, left". . ."open hatch". . . adjust speed, 120 knots, prepare 10 secs and on goes the red light. Slight bumps are felt as they leave the aircraft one by one. No wonder it seems lighter already: they had the most impressive collection of weapons and equipment and all looked like poachers with their pockets full.'

Suddenly the flight nearly came to a violent and fatal end. Another Albemarle flying at the same height and speed appeared almost in the same air space: an unexpected hazard of perfect navigation and flying. 'By instinct I kicked the big aircraft hard over almost onto its back and missed him by a hair's breadth. The last passenger who should have gone was thrown back in, on to the roof – it was the boss soldier, too.

'How we missed the other aircraft we shall never know. This was no night to go round again as all hell now let loose. A tight circle and back again and our last passenger was out. We can now open up, go down low and beat a retreat.'

It was a successful night's work and the lieutenant in command of their 'guests' survived his aerial misadventure and the fighting that followed. He showed his appreciation: 'The boss soldier brought our crew a memento back and news that they duly put out the markers.'

Leonard Archer and his crew landed back at base in the early hours of D-Day and a few hours later were airborne again on another operation, codenamed Mallard.

Flight Lieutenant Oliver Kingdon was another Albemarle pilot. His Squadron, No 295, was stationed at Harwell. He took part in both the paratroop drop on the night of 5/6 June and Operation Mallard. Of the former, he writes: 'The first member of the Allied forces to land in Normandy on 6 June, 1944, was Lieutenant Bobby de la Tour of the Parachute Regiment. He commanded a small detachment [a stick] of ten Pathfinders whose job was to lay out patterns of lights in a small field to guide the following waves of parachutists and gliders from the British 6th Airborne Division. A few months earlier he had been in a musical on the London stage.'

Like all six crews on the operation, his had been selected for 'this honour and responsibility' because they excelled at their profession. His navigator, Sergeant Alan Muddiman, was 'a man with exceptional night vision and map-reading skills who was the equivalent of the bomb aimer in a bombing aircraft. It was he who had to guide us over the last few thousand yards and give the signal for the parachutists to jump so that they landed on precisely the right spot.

'We crossed the French coast near Ouistreham in pale moonlight and, using the aerial photographs which we had been studying for many hours, flew at 500ft to the small field which had been designated our dropping zone. The signal was given and our men jumped just as the German anti-aircraft batteries opened up. Then came a message on the intercom that the sergeant who was to jump last had fouled his lines and had not gone. I told the crew we would go round again and our excellent map-reader navigated us back over the same field and the sergeant jumped. We heard later that Bobby de la Tour had been killed in action two weeks after the landing.'

Oliver Kingdon is one of the few air crew who ever knew in detail what happened to the paratroops they dropped. After a lapse of thirty-nine years he learned that the sergeant who was second-in command of the stick had landed only a few feet from his officer and had been able to pull him out of the mud in a small duck pond in which he had landed and might have drowned.

He remarks, 'It was a fantastic feat of accurate dropping on the part of Alan Muddiman – to land two men so close together several minutes apart at night, in a strong wind and under fire.'

It is generous of Leonard Archer and Oliver Kingdon to give all the credit for the success of their sorties that night to their navigators, but an air crew works as a team and it takes an above average or exceptional pilot to fly accurate courses consistently in difficult conditions.

It was Kingdon's air gunner, Sergeant Bill Hulme, who, in correspondence in 1983 with Mr W. R. Ramage, the former paratroop sergeant, found out the details of the drop and landing.

Ramage wrote, 'This is the first chance I've had to say thanks for our safety to all the crew. Your letter makes me aware that it was team work that got us there.

'You will remember the last time you saw me I was going through the jumping exit with my kitbag in my hand – no time to strap it to my leg after No 9 kicked the "ditching belt", which tripped me up and with the weight I was carrying, around 90lb, I was like a sheep on its back. I can remember Douglas Worth, the *Daily Express* war reporter, and others helped me get through the exit. It was he who gave us the time of 0022 hrs as landing.

'I appeared to be able to see the *coup de main* gliders on their way to Ranville bridges. I was looking down over them about a quarter of a mile away to my left, lit on occasions by flashes from the coast. Just in no time at all I landed into a damn great Lombardy poplar tree. When I hit the ground I couldn't believe that I was still in one piece, but subconsciously I remembered which direction you took for home and knew if I walked in the opposite direction to find the stick and Bob, we were in business.

'The first thing I tried was my "handy talky". It must have been damaged on landing. Around this time in the half darkenss I saw and heard a herd of stampeding cattle led by a black and white bull. I threw the knackered "HT" at the leader, which hit it and they changed direction from me and went charging in circles all around the field.

'I knew there were no Germans lurking around in the midst of this stampede – that gave me all-round protection. The leader came back again but didn't charge. The password was Punch and Judy for that night, so I went to find a Punch or Judy. I came to what looked like piles of pit props and beyond a boggy pond, I moved up to the timber piles as I was becoming aware that someone was in the bog and saying "Punch". I answered "Judy". I knew it was Bobby by his voice. He was not far in from the side, so I found a long pole in the timber and pulled him out. All this took time and shortened our time to target. We came over the remainder of the stick in a hedgerow, calmly smoking, eight of them all told. I think they could be excused for this with their leaders coming from one direction that had not been practised. Fate was on our side – Bobby would have slipped under the mud so easily, especially with the weight he was carrying.

'I rousted everybody up and got them moving. We came to a flooded ditch, about 15ft wide, depth unknown. This had not been considered in our timetable to the DZ. We had only our toggle ropes to get everything across. When they were linked together they made a rope of about 20ft. I took the end, lunged for the other side and got everyone over.

'Around this time one of our stick broke his leg and had to be left as we were getting behind with these stoppages and had to press on. When we reached the DZ troops began to arrive quickly on top of us as we had time to put out two lights and a Eureka [type of radar beacon] in position. The smoke from the bombs around the battery was drifting across the field and the hunting horn was audible, gathering the 9th together and the Canadian Company to their objectives.

'After a while we set off in the direction of the hard standing to set up the lamps for the glider assault on the fort. By this time our back-up stick had reached us. We moved off with members of the reconnaissance party leading. Half-way there a German patrol crossed our path but didn't see us.

'The three gliders meant for the assault on the fort were in a spot of bother: one had tow rope trouble in England, one landed a distance away, the third landed in an orchard. When we helped them out they were a bit "shook up". No one landed in the fort.

'I'm quickly passing through this phase of the attack on the fort. It was found on the capture of the guns they were a much smaller calibre than expected. I read in an account of the attack that the range would have been of no danger to the beach and referred to as "extra insurance", also recaptured by the enemy three days later.

'After the attack approximately 80 men left Le Plain following hedges and lanes to the west of Goneville. The biggest danger of this phase was being bombed with AP by our own planes and that we had to use yellow silk strip as recognition when they appeared in a set area and which we had to pass through.

'We met a Frenchman at Hauger who warned that approximately 200 soldiers of the Oust Battalion were in the area. It was supposed to be holed up in a château, but no one on either side knew the strength of the other. A patrol was put against them, but it failed.

'We had a go at them as we were approaching Le Plain from the battery, by removing pantiles from the roof and firing Bren guns and rifles through the gaps. They responded quite strongly. Most of them were Russians, Poles and others under the command of German oficers and NCOs who had told them that, if captured, they would be shot. No matter, we were ordered to break off this action, so it came to nothing.

'The weather took a turn for the better, lovely sunny day ensued. One of our L/C was shot by snipers and there was another patrol. Anyway we passed the afternoon behind the 4ft garden wall of the château d'Armaville. The 6th Commando were supposed to reach us around 1300 hrs, but the going was heavy from the beaches and they didn't reach us until 1600 hrs. They liquidated the situation and 25 Russians with 3 MGs were captured.

'We had tea, then set off for Ranville – what a stroll that was. We never saw any enemy till we reached a quarry where the Div Ammunition Dump was being set up. A line of captured prisoners – what a mixture! Aggressive to the last, one spat on someone in defiance. The impression that they were all a lot of pushovers because they were Russians, Poles, Lithuanians commanded by German officers and NCOs was all a myth.

'We arrived at Ranville around 2000 hrs and dug in as the reserve to General Gale's HQ. Around 2100 hrs the Germans put down a barrage when the Air Landing Brigade came in in their gliders. We lost another officer, wounded through the knees and evacuated.

'That for me was D-Day, so I settled into a foxhole for the night.'

There is a special purpose in including this account in these pages, which are principally concerned with air operations. It is impossible to calculate fairly the comparative dangers on active service in the various military arms, despite casualty statistics. Most people would probably agree that the infantry and tank and armoured car crews are at the greatest risk. It is equally invidious to try to assess the risks incurred by each of the armed forces. But it is possible to compare their hardships. Sailors were vulnerable to attack by aircraft, submarines or surface vessels at any hour of the day or night, but slept in reasonable comfort and fed comparatively well.

The greatest contrast is between airmen and soldiers, which the paratroop sergeant's unadorned account illustrates. Goodness knows how many days after being dropped into action he and his comrades were able to have a bath or even wash, to sleep on a mattress, to change their clothes or eat three good hot meals on the same day. For the air crews who flew the paras and gliderborne troops to the battle zone, the diverse dangers inherent in flying in a large formation and being shot at by flak – and one's own naval and military anti-aircraft on the way home – were of fairly short duration; and once back at base, all the amenities of civilized living were at hand. If it was of any interest – it could hardly be of any comfort – to the men they left behind on the battlefield, air crews were not unaware of such good fortune as they enjoyed.

Squadron Leader R. G. Woodman DSO DFC, of 169 Squadron, 100 Group, was also in the vanguard of the immediate pre-invasion operations. The squadron flew countermeasure Mosquitos fitted with Mk IV radar and Serrate, the device that could home on to enemy night fighters. It could detect them at up to sixty miles when the enemy aircraft was ahead and approaching, at five miles' range when the target was astern and at various ranges on other bearings.

D-Day had been planned for 5 June and 'Tim' Woodman and his observer, Flying Officer P. Kemmis, were detailed for a special operation on the night of 4–5 June, but weather forced the invasion to be postponed for twenty-four hours. At about 2200 on 5 June they took off from Great Massingham, in Norfolk, to patrol from west of Paris towards the Cherbourg peninsula, hunting for enemy night fighters that might spot the invasion forces crossing the Channel.

To avoid entering over Normandy he flew out over the North Sea, as though heading for Germany, down across Belgium and round the south of Paris. His patrol line was from west of Paris, north-west to within ten or twenty miles of the D-Day landing beaches. There they patrolled until just before dawn. They were concerned that German night fighters might be alerted to Allied activity on the coast and would fly there and, as he says, 'perhaps discover that a massive invasion was taking place across the Channel. It was imperative that I intercept such aircraft and shoot them down. My observer kept his head glued to the radar, but there was no reaction from the Germans.

'There were towering cumulo-nimbus thunder clouds flitting by from the west and these I flew round at heights of 12,000 to 20,000ft. There was some searchlight activity up the coast and some flak, but nothing like we had experienced over Germany. No German night fighters got airborne: only two pilots, one a Hauptmann, the other an NCO, in day fighters after dawn. I was not permitted to fly back to the UK over the beaches but had to go back the same way as I had come – over Belgium, where it had become broad daylight.

'We flew at 20,000ft with my observer keeping a constant lookout behind. I certainly expected to see German day fighters flying west towards the beaches, but there was no sign of any enemy activity. I could tangle with a single Me109 in a Mosquito, but not with two or more and there was no cloud cover.

So I was relieved to get across the coast and out over the North Sea. We began to wonder if the invasion had been cancelled again after we had taken off.' He had had to keep radio silence all the time and had heard nobody else on the air.

'But as we approached the Norfolk coast we realized the invasion must be on, as every USAAF aeroplane in Norfolk seemed to be taking to the skies: formations climbing up all over the place like skeins of wild duck. After being de-briefed we sat down to our night flying supper-cum-breakfast and listened to the news of the invasion on the radio.

'The entry in my logbook is: "Quietest night of the year".'

There is an item of information to add to the foregoing which, although it has no direct connection with the invasion, is a valuable explanation of a phenomenon seen by many pilots and crews at night.

The USAAF was keen to learn about Serrate, so an American pilot was attached to the squadron. After having been trained in the use of the equipment, he returned early from his first operation with the excuse that he had been intercepted by three FW190s. As these flew only by day and operated in pairs of multiples of two, and as his observer had not seen them nor had the radar picked them up, the reception of this was sceptical. On his second operation he turned back from Aachen on being caught by searchlights. He took evasive action and both he and his observer reported having been intercepted by balls of light that followed his every movement.

This latter statement introduces 'Tim' Woodman's clarification of a misconception. He says, 'I took the observer up in a Mosquito and demonstrated to him: when violently manoeuvring a Mosquito, you obtain wingtip vortices, visible as swirling vapour. Illuminated by searchlights, they appear to be balls of light following one's every manoeuvre. The observer agreed. The American captain was sent back to the USAAF as unsuitable material for RAF Serrate operations.'

Associated with the Second World War, invasions suggest cordial, efficient co-operation between the fighting Services of the Allied nations. It was never thus, except for the virtually unopposed landings in the south of France on 15 August, 1944. After the display of vanity by, and antagonism between, the most publicized British and American Generals during the Italian campaign, it was obvious that similar egotistical histrionics bred by ambition and conceit would provoke quarrels in high command, with resultant disorder. At all levels the invasion of Normandy was no impeccable exhibition of a carefully planned operation being put into practice. At about the time when the first British paratroops landed in France, human error – less tactfully, muddle and inefficiency – began to flaw the great venture.

On the night of 5/6 June, 1944, hundreds of bombers were on their way back from targets in France. Flight Sergeant Douglas Schofield, who had joined the RAF as an observer, later renamed navigator, was flying as bomb aimer in a No 15 Squadron Lancaster piloted by an Australian, Flight Sergeant Upton.

He recalls, 'It was around three in the morning, pitch dark as we crossed the Channel and were already beginning to lose altitude on what should have been a quiet night.' The aircraft was at about eight or ten thousand feet when, 'suddenly, without warning, all hell broke loose below and flak came up at us from the sea. At least two Lancasters were shot down in our view, a terrible thing to happen. It was only when we landed that we found out that D-Day had just started,' a tribute to the excellence of security. Not so reassuring was the fact that, when the crew reported what had happened, the Intelligence officers 'had no clues'.

Even more disturbing for the prospects of competent liaison and concerted action between the Allies was the rider. 'We were informed that the US Navy was to blame. They got their codes wrong, or something like that. An apology came through from the Head of the US Navy about five days later. In the meantime two fine crews had been lost. As we were usually kept in the dark about everything, it might have been more, I have never forgotten this "accident" because our aircraft missed it by inches.' He later transferred to another crew and it was in accordance with the statistics for Bomber Command expectation of life that, 'Upton was shot down after about ten operations over France with the entire crew except myself. There were no survivors.'

It was not only Bomber Command's friendly neighbourhood allies who frequently proved as lethal as the enemy. Flight Sergeant W. E. Barker was the rear gunner in a Lancaster of 75 (New Zealand) Squadron, who says: 'The thing I remember most about D-Day [it was past midnight on D-Day eve by the time they were returning] is leaving the coast of France in cloud. We came out of the cloud and I saw two Halifaxes also coming out of the cloud right behind us. As they came out of the cloud they smashed into each other and both went down, and as we were very low they went straight into the sea.'

These episodes, like similar ones repeated many times during the night and eary morning hours immediately preceding the Normandy landings and the succeeding weeks, encapsulate the truth about all warfare – above all, combined operations by air, sea and land. When not only different Services but also divers nations are allied, there lies the greatest potential for confusion. In this instance there were two nations nearly all of whose characterstics were opposed. In theory they had a common language, but in practice the form of its usage by the younger nation was so vitiated that it was sometimes incomprehensible. On one side of the Atlantic was a people whose history covers two millennia, whose habits are frugal, its style modest, its armed forces devoted to precision of aim and economy of resources in numbers of men and weapons. From the far side of the ocean came a nation only a couple of centuries old, its manner brash, its habits extravagant and boastful, its military performance reliant on sheer weight of numbers and fire power however ill-directed. A swift and proficient advance from the shores of France to Berlin was as likely as a chess grand master partnered by the heavyweight boxing champion of the world winning the Wimbledon men's doubles against a pair who had held the title for years.

★

At midnight on D-minus-one the RAF dropped 200 dummy paratroops at Yvetot, thirty miles south-west of Dieppe; 200 more were dropped near the base of the Cotentin Peninsula, another fifty, east of the River Dives and fifty also south-west of Caen. They were accompanied by the wire recorders that broadcast the sounds of battle. The RAF also dropped SAS parties near Yvetot and on the Cotentin Peninsula, who went into action as soon as the dummies touched down. Forty aircraft, Hudsons, Stirlings and Halifaxes, of which two did not return, made these deliveries. The operation was of far greater importance than its small scale, compared with the numbers on a bombing raid or glider-towing mission, suggests. The SAS had orders to allow some of the enemy troops they engaged to escape, so that they would spread alarm by reporting a landings by hundreds of paratroops.

In almost every way that misdirection of the enemy's attention was done, the RAF played the major part. Misleading him about where the landings were to be made was a task concurrent with softening up the real intended area. For every bomber or fighter-bomber attack on the future beachheads and their adjacent terrain, and for every photographic or visual reconnaissance sortie over this area, two were flown over the Pas de Calais. Twice as many tons of bombs were dropped on coastal batteries north of Le Havre as on those to the west of it.

During the short final period of preparation for the landings the RAF flew 53,200 sorties – 24,600 by Bomber Command and 28,600 by 2nd TAF. Together they dropped 94,200 tons of bombs. The USAAF's sorties totalled 142,000 and bomb tonnage dropped 101,200.

The disparity between the ratios of sorties to bomb tonnage was owed to the RAF aeroplanes' greater bomb load than the USAAF's. A Lancaster's was one 22,000lb or 14,000lb of smaller boms. A Halifax's was 13,000lb. A B17 Flying Fortress's was 6,000lb.

The RAF was addicted to singing a mocking ditty to the tune of 'John Brown's Body': 'We fly our Flying Fortresses at twenty thousand feet, (repeated three times)/But we've only got a tiny little bomb.'

Sung in any bar where members of the USAAF were present, it provoked fisticuffs – and it was not a uniquely Bomber Command display of derision. A rugged young officer of Coastal Command is remembered to have spent an unduly long time in the 'convenience' of a favourite RAF pub. When he rejoined his companions there was a swelling under his eye. 'What kept you?' He was asked. 'Well . . . there was a Yank in there,' he explained. 'And you sang "Tiny Little Bomb"?' 'Yes.' 'Where is he? You should buy him a drink.' The flying officer, who had boxed middleweight for a civilian club and various Service teams, was renowned for a double punch, left hooks to the body and head, that would have dropped a horse. 'He's on his feet again, but still in the bog, trying to stop his nose bleeding. It'd drip into his beer.'

The B17 was armed with thirteen 0.5 machine guns. The Lancaster carried ten .303s and the Halifax only nine. The RAF was also prone to another provocative habit – recitation of a composition, in what was thought to be an American Southern accent, which was also a stirrer up of physical remonstration. 'In mah ship, evrahbody's got a gurn, except the co-pilot. And he got so goddam mad, he went right out and gotten himself a gurn. So now, in mah ship, evrahbody's got a gurn.'

Casualties on operations, however, were no matter for goading or jest. During the nine weeks immediately preceding D-Day the RAF lost 702 aircraft, the USAAF, 1,251 – which meant over 12,000 American lives.

By the time D-Day arrived, the British and Americans had done disabling damage to the Germans' means of mobility in France. Many of the targets were suggested by the French Resistance groups. The main ones were railway marshalling yards and tracks, which disrupted the movement of troops and war materials. Similar targets were also severely damaged in Belgium.

5

THE FRENCH RESISTANCE ORGANIZATION

In France preparations for the landing had been keeping pace with the preliminary operations by the Allied air forces for months before D-Day.

On the withdrawal of the British Expeditionary Force from France in 1940, over 40,000 British troops were left behind. They were still there on 29 June, 1940, when the armistice between France and Germany became effective.

The first seeds of what would grow into a country-wide Resistance organization were sown immediately by French families who sheltered hundreds of them and tried to help them to return home.

Radio contact with London was soon established and in 1941 the first active units to fight the Germans secretly were formed – the *Maquis*. This word was chosen because it meant 'wild, bushy country', which described the terrain in which thousands of the underground fighters hid, had their headquarters and kept their armouries. Every unit had a code name. One was called Foch, in honour of the revered *Maréchal* of the Great War.

Since the night of 19/20 October, 1940, Lysanders of the RAF Special Duties Squadron had been flying in and out of France, depositing and picking up spies, radio operators and other British and French members of the Resistance. As the time approached when an Allied invasion was expected as the next logical step towards Germany's defeat, liaison between England and the Resistance leaders became busier.

Jean Fargeas belonged to the *Maquis* Bir Hacheim, in Charente, which covered Cognac, Angoulême, Confolens and Cha-
banais. His wife was English, so, as he puts it, 'We therefore
experienced certain difficulties, as you can easily imagine,
throughout the occupation. It was thanks to the good deeds of
sincere friends that we were able to fight and emerge with our
lives in 1945. Liaison was constant with the RAF, USAAF and
Canadians, by radio, by small aeroplanes [Lysanders] and small
boats that sailed from Breton fishing ports to the south coast of
England.'

It is the British who are regarded as the most habitual
exponents of understatement. Monsieur Fargeas's dismissive
description of life under the merciless German occupation is a
masterly exercise of that proclivity. Also, his modest summary
omits one essential detail – that he could have avoided being there.

When the first troops of the British Expeditionary Force had
landed at Cherbourg on 10 September, 1939, Jean Fargeas was
one of the French liaison officers there to greet them. He
remained with the BEF throughout all its vicissitudes, from the
so-called *drôle de guerre*, or, as the American journalists called it,
the Phoney War, through the fighting that began on 10 May,
1940, to the retreat across Belgium to Dunkirk and other French
ports. At midnight on 1 June, 1940, he went aboard a British
cruiser that was torpedoed twice on the passage to Margate,
which took eleven hours owing to fog.

The British and French Expeditionary Forces to Norway
withdrew to Scotland on 7 June, 1940. From there the French
force moved to Liverpool, where Jean Fargeas joined them to
await re-embarkation for home. Next, joined now by other
interpreters, the French were transferred to Tidworth where
they were given food and toilet necessities – they had lost all
their possessions except their paybooks, which were sewn to
their underclothes. Through the Red Cross they had sent word
to their families that they were in England. On orders from the
French Embassy in London, they set off for Weymouth on 10
June, made a night crossing and reached Cherbourg at five
o'clock next morning during an air raid by Ju87s.

Jean Fargeas writes: 'Shortly after landing we had a cup of coffee, then were sent on our way to Caen, where the worn-out shoes in which we had marched more than 800 kilometres on the way to Dunkirk were replaced. Other musterings took place in Normandy and Brittany before we set off southwards.'

His English wife was awaiting him in France of course, but it was still a brave decision to return home rather than stay in England and try to arrange for her to join him there.

The name of the *Maquis* with which he operated was chosen in honour of a desert battle, the first opportunity the French Army had had to fight the Germans since France surrendered two years previously. In May, 1942, the *Afrika Korps* attacked the Allied front that extended south from Gazala, on the Libyan coast, to a desert spot called Bir Hacheim, which was held by General Koenig's 1st Free French Brigade. The air and land fighting around this southern strongpoint lasted for two weeks and was so ferocious that the area became known as The Cauldron. The French fought with great gallantry and spirit. When the enemy was finally repulsed, their General signalled Air Vice Marshal Coningham, in command of Desert Air Force, '*Bravo! Merci pour la RAF*'; to which the reply came, '*Bravo à vous! Merci pour le sport.*' The Maquis showed the same zest for a fight and the same hunger for revenge.

The main signals traffic between London and the Resistance was about the delivery of arms and the selection of targets. For years the RAF and later also the USAAF had dropped personnel, weapons and other supplies by parachute. Now the requirements increased. Jean describes how the dropping zones were marked. 'At the moment for which the drop was timed, in the depth of night, the *Maquis* switched on torches at the four corners of a square or oblong area of flat ground, sometimes a hilltop.'

On the night of 5/6 April, 1944, the Bir Hacheim *maquisards* were waiting for a Halifax of 644 Squadron bringing equipment that would be used after the Normandy landings to help prevent the enemy retreating as the Allied armies advanced. The pilot was flighte Lieutenant R. F. W. Cleaver, DSO, for whom that night's operation was to earn him a DFC. His navigator, Flight

Sergeant Alan Matthews, was soon to find himself adding the Bir Hacheim badge to his uniform and, for the next six months, firing a Bren or Sten machine gun instead of an aircraft's Brownings.

While the aircraft was approaching the dropping zone, flak hit and stopped both starboard engines, one of which caught fire. The captain ordered his crew to bale out, then risked his own life by making a hasty crash landing in an aircraft loaded with ammunition and explosives. Alan Matthews alighted in the Charente River. He could not swim, but his life jacket kept him afloat and when he clambered out he was lucky enough to make contact with the *Maquis*.

The principal targets that the Resistance asked to be bombed were railway marshalling yards, stations, locomotives and rolling stock. Many of their own activities were attacks on troop trains and sabotage of railway tracks. After the landings, when the Germans began to retreat, the main function of the Resistance was to delay them by every means, including pitched battles. If captured, they were not treated as prisoners of war, they were tortured and shot.

Several Canadians from Quebec, bilingual in French and English, were among the volunteers for service with the Resistance. Allyre Sirois, aged nineteen, was one of them. He parachuted into the Angoulême area in 1944 as a radio operator and organizer of groups numbering twelve to fifteen, in the Buckmeister *Maquis*. They lived a normal civilian life by day and carried on their sabotage and intelligence gathering by night. Between April and August, 1944, Sirois made 180 radio transmissions to England and arranged for eighty arms drops, an impressive scale of activity. On a visit to his old comrades and their families in 1983, he said, in an interview with the Press, 'Before the start of a mission we were given a life expectancy of six weeks. I lasted six months. I changed my whereabouts every fortnight and my radio frequencies every fifteen minutes.'

6

D-DAY

'Invasion' has a dashing connotation. It incites images of naval
bombardment pulverizing enemy coastal defences, of tanks
and infantry storming ashore from landing craft that have carried
them to the beach, to crush all opposition under an irresistible
tidal wave of fighting men and armour, bayonets and bullets.

The reality is of underwater obstacles – mines, and steel posts
set in concrete – that hinder or tear the bottom out of the assault
craft. Many vessels have to unload their passengers and
armoured vehicles into the water, to wade, swim and churn
their way to land. More mines, barbed wire and concrete
'dragon's teeth' await the attackers on the level sand and the
dunes beyond. From reinforced concrete strongpoints, gun
emplacements and trenches that have escaped destruction, rifle,
machine gun and artillery fire sweep the beach and the inshore
waters. Mortars and hand grenades scatter shards of sharp,
searingly hot steel fragments. Men are killed and wounded
before they even reach the shore or after their first few strides
across the killing ground.

On D-Day the weather did not grant the invaders any favours,
whether they landed from the air or by sea, dropped bombs or
patrolled over the combat zone. The clouds were low and along
the Normandy coast the wind was gusty; the waves were six
feet high.

Four years and nine months of war (for the USA, two and a
half years) had bred among the RAF and Commonwealth air
forces a battle-hardened nucleus of experienced fighter and

bomber pilots and crews among whom many had, inherently or acquired, that essential quality – leadership. Some were now in action over Burma or Italy, but there was still a sufficient number of talented leaders for the Normandy operations.

The most renowned wing leader by that time was Wing Commander J. E. J. 'Johnny' Johnson DSO DFC and bar (later Air Vice Marshal CB CBE and with two bars to his DSO). He already had thirty confirmed kills and was to add eight more during the next three and a half months. He ended the war as, officially, Britain's and the Commonwealth's highest scorer of the war. There is another contender for the distinction, Squadron Leader M. T. St J 'Pat' Pattle DFC and bar, who did all his fighting in North Africa and Greece. He was credited with at least forty victories and is believed to have reached fifty – but his squadron's records were lost in the Greek campaign and the helter-skelter retreat from Crete. Whatever Pattle's score, it must be said that his victims were mostly Italian Fiat CR42 biplane fighters that were no match for his Hurricane, whereas all Johnnie's were Me109s or FW190s and a Me110.

Wing Commander Johnson had commanded a Canadian wing for six months in 1943 and now had command of another, 144 Wing of 83 Group, 2nd Tactical Air Force. It comprised 441 (Silver Fox), 442 (Caribou) and 443 (Hornet) Squadrons, Royal Canadian Air Force, flying Spitfire IXs.

Shortly before dawn on the apocalyptic day he led the wing off the ground from Ford, on the Sussex coast. He wrote: 'From the pilot's viewpoint, flying conditions were quite reasonable – better than we expected after the gloomy forecasts of the previous two or three days. The cloud base was about 2,000 feet and the visibility between five and six miles.' But with hundreds of aircraft crossing the Channel in both directions at the same time and only 2,000ft between sea and sky, precise formation keeping and accurate flying made a heavy mental and physical demand.

Most wings that operated that day were, in Johnnie Johnson's words, 'sniffed at' by USAAF P47 Thunderbolts or P38 Lightnings, whose pilots made a dart at every formation they saw, in the hope that it would be an enemy. No 144 Wing's leader has recorded that '. . . a wing of American Thunderbolts harried our progress and for a few uneasy moments we circled warily round each other. Formations of allied aircraft had attacked each other during the preceding months, but in this instance recognition was soon effected.'

The wing flew four patrols over the beachhead 'and never a sign of the *Luftwaffe*'.

All the pilots had made at least one sortie and when the day's stint was done they were 'very quiet: it was apparent that they were bitterly disappointed with the *Luftwaffe's* failure to put in an appearance'. The same mood of anticlimax and frustration was evident in every fighter wing that had operated. 'We had geared ourselves for a day of intense fighting.' There was plenty to come.

The USAAF's contribution to events on D-Day morning was somewhat marred when a force of 480 B24s (Liberators) carrrying 1,285 tons of bombs were supposed to bomb Omaha beach through cloud, on instruments. Their orders were not to attack until they had crossed the coast. In consequence, the first bombs fell a few hundred yards inland and the rest were spread over three miles. Instead of pulverizing the beach defences, they did considerable execution among the French population and farm animals.

The *Luftwaffe*, which had only 153 serviceable bombers based in northern France, Belgium and Holland, and a mere 119 serviceable fighters near the Channel coast, flew 319 sorties, of which only a handful were over the Normandy beaches. Goering had been waiting for signs that an invasion was imminent before moving fighters from Germany to the battle area, but deception was so successful that the Germans were taken by surprise. Even had the enemy's air defence been stronger, it would not have been adequate; whereas the RAF and USAAF mustered over 5,000 fighters based in Britain, the total German day fighter strength was 1,789.

The RAF and USAAF flew 15,004 sorties on D-Day in direct support of the invasion. Including heavy bombers and other types that indirectly contributed to the landings, the total of sorties flown between 2100 on D–minus–one to 2100 on D–Day was 25,275.

Although 9,210 aeroplanes were available on the eve of Operation Overlord, the effort by individual fighter pilots and bomber crews was intensive. Flight Sergeant W. E. Barker's logbook bears witness:-

'6.6.44. Hour 0115. Aircraft Type Lancaster. Daylight bombing Ouistreham (invasion). Flying time 3.45.

'6.6.44. Hour 2230. Aircraft Type Lancaster. Lisieux (France). Flying Time 3.25.'

Seven hours and ten minutes in the air, entailing one take–off in the small hours and another late the same night, plus the hours of pre–flight preparation, meant a heavy work load. Add the flak from the moment the crew crossed the French coast on their way out until they recrossed it on their homeward leg, as well as collision risk over the Channel and the target, and it makes an unlovely sum. Consider further the odds on being shot at by trigger–happy gunners on Allied naval vessels in the Channel of USAAF night fighters and similarly welcomed by anti–aircraft batteries along England's south coast, and one can appreciate the reality of what those entries in an air gunner's logbook stood for.

On a later operation, to bomb oil storage plants at Basse near Bordeaux, he recalls; 'This meant flying very low on leaving England so that we could not be seen on radar. I remember looking up at the coast of Cornwall and scaring the life out of a man on a horse who arrived at the top of a hill at the same time as we flew over it just a few feet above him. We then had to fly just above sea level all the way to our target.' One second's lapse of the pilot's concentration could have sent the heavy aircraft diving under the sea.

Mention, five decades after the end of the war, that one was in the RAF and the response will probably be, 'Did you fly Spirtifes?' If not, then, 'Were you on fighters or bombers?' Coastal Command is seldom remembered, although its torpedo

Beauforts suffered the highest casualty rate of any. Its lightly armed twin-engine anti-submarine aircraft were easy prey for Me109s and 110s, FW190s, Ju88s and FW Condors. If, patrolling at 500ft, an engine failed, they probably sank without trace. That was why, although briefed to fly at that height, or 450ft in Wellingtons that had a radio altimeter, 750ft was the prudent, and preferred, minimum.

As for Transport Command, whose unarmed Dakotas carried paratroops and towed gliderborne assault forces on such attractive excursions as the Primosole Bridge, Normandy and Arnhem operations through raging flak and enemy fighters, it is probably thought of as an aerial freight delivery service. Who thinks of Flight Lieutenant Lord of 217 (Dakota) Squadron when RAF winners of the Victoria Cross are discussed?

The questioner's assumption is that you must have flown, presumably, fighters or bombers, and the implication is that if you did not you cannot have risked life and limb. The ground tradesmen and officers who served aboard Fighter Direction Tenders or in Servicing Commandos could disabuse the general ignorance.

Leading Aircraftman Peter Read was one of the many who were whisked away from service on dry land to the rigours of the sea, in a craft that rolled like a fiddler's bitch in heavy weather. His maritime misadventure began in January, 1944, with six weeks' vigorous training at a naval shore establishment in Ayrshire, HMS *Dundonald*, where he exchanged RAF blue for khaki battledress with the dark blue and red Combined Operations badge. He and his RAF shipmates, trained by Royal Marines instructors, practised going ashore from landing craft 'on to beaches frozen hard by frost'.

When he joined Fighter Direction Tender 216 – a converted landing ship, tank – lying off Dunoon, at the mouth of the Clyde, he found her 'the most ungainly vessel I had ever seen. Radar aerials like revolving chicken coops, RDF [radio direction finding] beacons, antennae for the Y Service'. This last had been formed in February, 1940, staffed by German-speaking RAF and WAAF personnel of all ranks. They listened to traffic between

Luftwaffe fighters and ground controllers and often interrupted to give false orders and information to the pilots.

On the tank deck were the filter room, where radar plots and visual observations were resolved into aircraft tracks, identified as friendly or hostile; the operations room, where these tracks were shown on a general situation map; and the ground controlled interception room, where controllers worked from echoes on their radar tubes, giving night fighter crews and day fighter leaders information about the position of their target and guiding them towards it.

The vessel was top-heavy. To counter this, part of her decks were covered with tons of pig iron ingots under steel mesh. Her armament was meagre: a four-inch gun and six 20mm Oerlikons. The improvisation aboard was complemented by Read's convoluted personal situation: 'The ship was provisioned by the Royal Navy and naval discipline was in force. So there was I, Royal Air Force, seconded to the Royal Artillery, on loan to Combined Operations and serving with the Royal Navy.'

March and April were spent off the Isle of Arran, 'working up and throwing up in about the same proportion,' while escorted by at least one corvette and two air/sea rescue high speed launches. FDT216 wallowed up the west coast of Scotland, around Cape Wrath and down the east coast to Sheerness, in Kent, thence 'to run the gauntlet through the Straits of Dover. My post was an observation platform abaft the main bridge to observe and report all movement and sound and visually identify all for the radar operators'. The voyage ended at Portland, among 'naval vessels of every nationality, who made some unkind remarks about our exotic appearance and inability to defend ourselves'.

Eric Ingham was a leading aircraftman radar operator in the same ship. The relationship between RAF and Navy was, he says, excellent throughout. He recalls that in the bows there was a Type 8F radar with sixty miles' range, which could read height as well as azimuth. Amidships a Type 11 centimetric radar picked up low-flying aircraft. On a lattice tower aft of the bridge was a navigational radar. Eight masts bore the aerials of VHF radio and beacons.

FTD216's station was to be off Omaha and Utah beaches. The RAF controlled Spitfires by day and Mosquitoes by night. American controllers handled the USAAF P47 Thunderbolts that gave daytime high level cover. Four wings, each comprising four Spitfire squadrons, whose main purpose was to keep enemy aircraft away from the beachhead, worked with her. Throughout the day one wing would be under control, another on its way out to take over, a third on its way back to base in England after finishing its stint, and a fourth being serviced.

In the early afternoon of 5 June the ship sailed, immediately astern of the minesweepers. LAC Peter Read was on deck, a lookout for enemy aircraft. LAC Eric Ingham was on watch in the operations room. All watertight doors were closed during darkness, so when he came off duty at midnight he 'had to kip down wherever I could', which meant the deck. Waking a couple of hours later he found the ship had stopped, bombs dropped by Lancasters were bursting along the French coast and flak in the sky.

Both men remember the turmoil, the noise and the macabre detail of the succeeding hours. Shells from USS *Arkansas* screamed overhead as she bombarded the shore. Landing craft surged past on the flood tide. Adrift on rafts, soldiers whose craft had been sunk called for help. Two climbed aboard and begged a Carley float from the captain, on which they paddled off to rejoin their unit. A badly wounded German pilot was picked up. His wounds and burns were tended to, but he died during the afternoon. When the tide turned, corpses and flotsam drifted past. All day USAAF bombers droned overhead but they saw no enemy aircraft.

Read says, 'That changed with the coming of night, when our night fighters brought down a number of German aeroplanes.'

It was about one o'clock on the morning of D-Day when he and his fellow lookouts saw a low-flying Ju88 appear suddenly in the moonlight, heading towards them. In the operations room, Ingham heard the warning that it was circling the ship, followed by the sound of the Oerlikons opening fire.

The next announcement was that a torpedo was running at them. 'There was a gigantic explosion and all the lights went out. A split second later the emergency lighting came on.'

On deck, Read remembers, 'Though the explosion was forward on the port side, the torpedo hit a diesel generator and exploded upwards, taking most of the deck pig iron with it, which came down with devastating effect.' After two hours in the water he was picked up and 'Two weeks later I spent my twenty-first birthday on survivor's leave.'

Five of the RAF were killed and twenty-five injured. There were no naval deaths.

Ingham was seated beside a controller, Flight Lieutenant Edwards, who, although the ship was listing sharply, did not move until he had called all the night fighters under control and told them to go over to other radio channels. For aircraftman and officer who had stayed at their posts, leaving the ship was made difficult by her steepening list as they struggled up wet, slippery ladders and decks. Luckily for Eric Ingham, he was a strong swimmer – a water polo player – for he spent over half an hour in the water without a life jacket before being picked up.

For one of the French squadrons in the RAF, No 345 (*Groupe Berry*), the war had contracted suddenly to the invasion area at 0435 on D-Day, when they took off with glimpses of the moon through gaps in drifting clouds as they raced between the runway lights. As for most of the other fighters airborne at that time, there was no dramatic encounter with the enemy. On the return Channel crossing, Lieutenant Joubert reported that he had engine trouble and was going to bale out. His leader, Captain Guizard, told Joubert's winger to stay with him. Joubert was seen to open his cockpit canopy as his Spitfire entered a layer of cloud at 3000ft. His dinghy was found some miles off Barfleur.

★

Flying Officer Leo Bulmer was a navigator in 21 (Mosquito) Squadron of 140 Wing in 2 Group 2nd TAF, which began its contribution to the invasion early in 1944. The squadron's standards were high: it had taken part in the raid when impeccable accuracy of timing and bomb-aiming blew down the walls of Amiens prison, which saved more than a hundred Frenchmen from execution. Until D-Day the squadron was on night intruder operations against enemy airfields, seeking to shoot down German aircraft as they took off or came in to land; making low-level attacks on V1 sites; and carrying out special operations against various Gestapo headquarters.

'From D-Day onwards,' he records, 'we were fully occupied in patrolling behind enemy lines at night, attacking trains, transport and anything that moved. We made low-level attacks where possible, which was a bit dodgy because it was all too easy to fly into the ground and we lost a few aircraft that way. We carried on where the Typhoons left off at dusk. We had an Army officer attached to us who briefed us on where the bomb line was and what enemy troop movements were expected. Usually we had a free hand to attack anything we liked within our chosen area but occasionally a particular target such as a bridge or road-rail junction would be specified.'

He makes a modest disclaimer that touches on one of the realities of operational flying: 'I never saw much of the action because it was my job to keep my eyes glued to the altimeter and read out the height to Ed [McQuarrie, of the Royal Canadian Air Force, his pilot] as we dived. We were supposed to pull out at 1000ft above the ground but I always added on another 500ft to be on the safe side. I did get it wrong on one occasion when the ground was higher than I'd anticipated and we felt an almighty thump as 2000lb of HE went off below us.'

His logbook entry for 6 June reads: 'Airborne 2345, duration 2.00 hrs. Patrolled Caen-Lisieux-Boisney road. No convoys, saw light in wood on outskirts of Lisieux, bombed from 1500ft. Results not seen. Bags of flak from ships in Channel, not aimed at us.'

He amplified: 'All aircraft were briefed to stay within a designated corridor when crossing the Channel. Outside of this, night fighters were patrolling with orders to shoot down any aircraft not within the corridor. As we left the English coast we saw flak coming up from a vessel in mid-Channel and one aircraft went down in flames; believe it was a four-engine kite [which meant that it could not have been German]. We decided to divert around that area and take a chance on the night fighters rather than get shot down by the Navy who, we believed, parked a ship(s) right on our corridor and, in true Navy fashion, shot at anything that came near.

'Our previous night ops had been intruders, where everything was in total darkness, so it came as a bit of a surprise when we got behind the beachhead to find lights all over the place. Most towns seemed to be in flames – Lisieux burned for several days.' He adds, with dispassionate practicality, 'It made navigation a lot easier.'

Having landed in the small hours of 7 June, he took off some twenty-four hours later on a sortie that lasted two hours and fifteen minutes. Of this his logbook records, 'Patrolled Caen-Argentan-Flers road. No convoys. Bombed railway bridge west of Ecouche. No results seen. No flak. Most of larger towns in flames.'

The Typhoon pilots, with their four 20mm cannon and 2000lb bomb load or eight 60lb rockets derived the gratest satisfaction from that day's work. While the interception Spitfires, Thunderbolts and Lightnings, guardians of the beachhead, ranged the sky fruitlessly seeking enemy aircraft to engage, the ground attack squadrons found no lack of targets.

Naval bombardment had knocked out most of the coastal strongpoints and 88mm gun emplacements, but there was still a formidable amount of machine gun and artillery fire falling on the beach and the vessels that lay close inshore. Fighter-bombers could attack them with greater accuracy than medium or heavy bombers or big naval guns. Inland, lorries rushing reinforcements to the battlefield were immune from attack except from

1. Squadron Leader Leonard Archer, a flight commander in 296 Squadron (see p.22).

2. Leonard Archer, with his wife, leaving Buckingham Palace after his investiture as a member of the Order of the British Empire.

3. Leading Aircraftman Oliver Kingdon, 1940.

4. Flight Lieutenant Kingdon, 1942 (see p.23).

5. Leading Aircraftman
Peter Read (see p.43).

6. Leading Aircraftman
Eric Ingham (see p.43).

7. B Squad, No. 3 Course, No. 36 OTU, Greenwood, Nova Scotia, September, 1943. Leo Bulmer is third from the left in the back row (see p.47).

8. 21 Squadron, Thorney Island, November, 1944.

the air – cannon sufficed for these – and tanks lumbering up to repel the invaders, for whom rockets were the most effective discouragement. Where buildings and railway yards were to be demolished, 500-pounders did the job efficiently.

The first enemy fighters over the beachhead had been a pair of FW190s that flashed across it at 1500 hrs and made off without firing their guns. A quarter of an hour later fifteen Ju88s flew over Gold Beach and were intercepted by 135 Wing, which claimed four destroyed and three damaged. Inland, at 1330, a squadron of Typhoons on reconnaissance had found a single FW190 and shot it down. Four more FW 190s arrived and made a pass at them from astern before disappearing. 164 Squadron's Typhoons spotted six Me109s while attacking a convoy, but no action was joined. Twelve Me109s appeared out of the low cloud soon after and shot down three out of twelve 183 Squadron Typhoons that were attacking tanks.

7

FRENCH AND BELGIAN
SQUADRONS IN THE RAF

For the French airmen, soldiers and sailors taking part D-Day – *Jour J* to them – was even more emotional than for their allies, to whom it also meant the hour of triumph, hope and vengeance.

> *'Chaque jour est un bien que du ciel je reçoi,*
> *Je jouis aujourd'hui de celui qu'il me donne . . .'*

'Each day is a boon I receive from Heaven, Today I enjoy the one it has given me.' When François Maucroix wrote those lines three centuries earlier he referred figuratively to the sky, but it had a literal meaning for the French bomber crews and fighter pilots who had waited four years to enjoy a return to their own shores and retribution on the enemy who had driven them into exile.

On the night of 5/6 June Bomber Command and No 100 (Bomber Support) Group flew 1335 sorties – 1136 of them against French coastal batteries. The men of all nationalities who had flown from England to bomb France and Germany did not know that, with the next dawn, Operation Overlord would be announced to the world; but some fighter pilots did.

Of the four all-French squadrons in the RAF, No 329 was the inheritor of the most distinguished record in *l'Aviation Militaire*, the original name of the French Air Force. It also inherited the most famous title, *les Cigognes*, the Storks – because this elongated and ungainly bird was depicted on the fuselage of its aeroplanes in the Great War of 1914–1918. In those days the number of a French squadron was preceded by the initial letter(s) of the aircraft it flew. This one's first was the Morane-Saulnier, so it began as MS3. In 1916 it changed to the Nieuport II (Bébé) and became N3. It ended the war as SPA3, flying Spads. In June, 1915, the famous Georges Guynemer joined the squadron and shot down 53 German aircraft before being killed in September, 1917. He was surpassed among Frenchmen only by René Fonck, of the same squadron – who survived the war and ended his career as a General – with 75, the greatest Allied ace. The third-highest-scoring French pilot, Charles Guynemer, 45 victories, was another *Cigognes* comrade.

These achievements must be assessed in perspective with those of the other leading fighter pilots on both the Allied and enemy sides. In the Royal Flying Corps, Major Edward ('Mick') Mannock was top scorer with 73 kills. The Canadian Lieutenant-Colonel William ('Billy') Bishop second, 72. Another Canadian, Major Raymond Collishaw, third, 68. Of the Germans, the order was Hauptmann Manfred Ritter von Richthofen, 80, Leutnant Ernst Udet, 52. Leutenant Erich Lowenhardt, 56. In the Italian Air Force: Maggiore Francesco Baracca, 36, Tenente Silvio Scaroni, 26, Maggiore Pier Piccio, 26. For the USA: Captain Edward Rickenbacker, 26, Second Lieutenant Frank Luke, 21, Major Raoul Lufbery, 17.

In the post-war *Armée de l'Air* the unit's number became 1/2, the 1st *excadrille* (squadron, but equivalent in size to a RAF flight) of the 2nd Fighter Regiment.

Disbanded in August, 1940, it was re-formed in Unoccupied France in July, 1941, and posted to Algeria. In 1942 it moved to Tunisia. In 1943 1/2 joined the Allies and, in early January, 1944, arrived in Britain, where it was equipped with the Spitfire VA. It was now *groupe Cigognes*, equivalent in numbers to an RAF squadron, and every officer and man serving in it was proudly aware of the tradition whose standards he had to maintain.

One of its pilots, reminiscing about D-Day, recalls: 'After having spent three months at RAF stations with permanent buildings, on 17 April, 1944, our wing moved to Merston, twenty-five kilometres east of Portsmouth. No longer were we in comfortable brick-built quarters, where smiling WAAFs brought us morning tea and polished our shoes. We lived in tents whose canvas afforded scant protection against the vagaries of the weather.

'Our thirty-gallon wing tanks were replaced by cylindrical forty-five gallon tanks that increased our range but reduced the aircrafts' speed, which made them unsuitable as interception fighters.'

It was tolerant of him not to denigrate these ungainly appendages, as most pilots did. The tanks were attached under a wing: as well as reducing speed, they not only made the aeroplane yaw dangerously on take-off, but also if a pilot had to make a wheels-up landing could be fatally disastrous. Drop tanks had been designed for use only when ferrying aeroplanes. Their use on operations was widely regarded as an aberration and imputed to the Air Ministry, where, it was popularly supposed, the Staff's knowledge of flying was minimal.

'On 3 June our ground crews began to paint black and white stripes on the wings and bands around the fuselage, to facilitate their identification during the operations over the Continent that appeared imminent. For weeks we had lived in tents near our aeroplanes. We were sure that a great event was in preparation. During our recent flights we had seen an immense assembly of all sorts of shipping along this part of the English coast and the innumerable troops ready to embark.

'On account of bad weather on 4 and 5 June, operations were cancelled. At 2130 hours on 5 June we assembled in the operations room and learned that tomorrow was to be *Jour J*. Our Wing [No 145 of 2nd Tactical Air Force, RAF] Operations Officer uncovered the wall map and we were amazed by what we saw. This news, so long awaited by all the pilots, aroused huge delight. Our hopes during four years of waiting were about to be realized: at last to see our families and tread our native soil again.

'This time [after cancellation on the two previous days] the invasion was on. On the map arrows made long tracks across the Channel from the Isle of Wight to the Normandy coast. The onslaught had been unleashed.'

'Throughout the late evening and early hours of the night we saw Dakotas flying low overhead, towing Horsa gliders that carried the troops who would parachute or land behind the enemy. It was difficult to close one's eyes that night.

'We flew twice that day over the landing beaches. The first time we took off, in the morning, we saw that for 180 kilometres the sea was crowded by an immense convoy of vessels. Thousands of aircraft filled the sky and we had to keep a sharp look out for them as well as keep formation. Christian Martell, who led the Wing, had warned us at briefing, "I don't want pilots watching the ground. Today you've got to scan the sky.".

'But the sky remained void of enemy aircraft that morning, at least for us. We were covering General Crerar's First Canadian Army on Sword and Juno beaches. The only danger was of collision with other aircraft in a small, crowded air space. The air umbrella was indeed open.

'Twice that day I shuttled back and forth over the Channel to the beachhead, a total of four flying hours. Ah! How happy I was after so long a wait and after having left my young wife and our nine-months-old baby in France two years earlier. I had not left in vain. And now, with these Canadians coming to liberate us, we were in a way protected by our own.' Why he apparently assumed that the greater part of Crerar's force was French Candian is obscure.

Also descended from SPA3, the former 2/2 *groupe Berry*, was now 345 Squadron RAF. It was commanded by Commandant (Squadron Leader) Jean Accart, who had left his wife and five children in France in October, 1943. By then the Germans had taken over the former Unoccupied Zone, so he had to escape by the same means as hundreds of shot-down RAF and USAAF air crew – on foot across the Pyrenees. He had seen a lot of action during the Battle of France in 1940 and was credited with sixteen victories. The French, however, had a typically insouciant, sceptical and entirely Gallic attitude to official statistics. It was their custom to allow a pilot the figure he claimed, but qualify it (one can vizualise the shrug) parenthetically: in this instance, '16 (12 *homologués* – officially confirmed)'. The RAF differentiates more strictly between the two categories and has a third – damaged: in the Gallic view, perhaps, that is a mere stuffy British scruple.

The other French squadrons in the RAF were 340 (*Ile de France*) and 341 (*Alsace*). The latter had the longest association with the RAF. In June, 1940, a few air and ground crew officers and ORs of *l'Aviation Militaire* stationed in Syria flew to Egypt to join the Free French forces, rather than serve in the German-controlled Vichy Government forces that were about to fight the British. RAF HQ in Cairo posted them to form a French flight in 274 Squadron, whose numbers were soon made up by more escapers from French territory. Early in 1941 the French flight was transferred to 73 Squadron. After two years' fighting in the desert, by which time the French pilots were flying Hurricanes, their flight was disbanded and they were sent to Britain to form 341 Squadron and fly Spitfires.

No 345's Operations Record Book describes what it calls the 'morning of revenge' in the breathless journalese style inherent in the historic present tense. 'The sky is empty of enemy aeroplanes. The flak is intense north of Caen. The pilots can see the prodigious enactment of the air, sea and land operation being carried out from the Orne to the east coast of Cotentin. On landing back at base, they deplore the regardless attitude of the French population who, in the midst of battle, wander about watching the sky instead of taking shelter in their cellars: for example, a woman in a red frock who was imprudently walking along the Manerbe-Lisieux road a hundred metres from a tank the Spitfires were attacking.

'At 2000 hrs the Wing flys its fourth mission of the day. It is to escort a train of gliders that are going to reinforce the airborne troops who landed last night. Although there is little attraction in being sheepdog to a flock over the Channel, above all in line astern [with a smaller separation between aircraft than when in finger four, because of poor visibility at that hour], a fantastic spectacle awaits us at the beachhead. Each towing aeroplane is going to turn before Caen, then climb towards the sea and the Orne canal, to release its glider which is going to land on one side or other of the canal in a sector held by the Germans. Hardly have they touched down when men leap out of them and, kneeling or lying prone, open fire. Light flak [the narrator means in calibre – 20mm] of terrible intensity shoots from the woods where it is camouflaged and from barges on the Orne. Some aeroplanes are hit and fall in flames, a glider catches fire, others break up on hitting the ground; but every ten or twenty seconds twenty machine guns arrive to reinforce the attackers. One of the boats on the Orne is too nasty. Wing Commander Compton, followed by his squadron, settles its account. After twenty minutes the Spitfires return to the sheepfold.'

Wing Commander W. V. Crawford-Compton, DSO (and bar) DFC (and bar), a New Zealander credited with 21½ victories, commanded 145 Wing from April, 1944, to May, 1945. He has been described as New Zealand's most highly decorated fighter pilot. In fact this distinction belongs to Group Captain Colin Gray, DSO (and bar) DFC (and two bars) whose confirmed tally was 27½.

Writing forty years after the event, General Charles Christienne of *l'Armée de l'Air* began his description of events on *Jour J* with the trite statement that 'If the earth of Normandy retains the mark of the hard fighting that took place there, the sky above the landing beaches reveals no trace of the aircraft that ploughed their way across it to assure the safety of the allied troops during the greatest military enterprise of all time.' What did he expect: wreckage magically suspended in the air, as it would have been in outer space? He continues: 'However, if you look carefully at the commemorative plaque on Omaha Beach you can see that it indicates the direction in which a Boston III of *groupe Lorraine*, whose task was to spread a smoke screen intended to hide American armour from the German guns, disappeared into the waves.

'The three men in the crew, Sergeant Boissieu, pilot, Second Lieutenant Camut, navigator and Sergeant Hasson, air gunner, were the three first French airmen brought down – at dawn on 6 June. It was not the German Air Force that did it.' But he does not tell us who or what did (probably flak), or whether the Boston flew into the sea – the most common of low-flying accidents. If it was flak, then he was wrong, for the German anti-aircraft artillery was an arm of the *Luftwaffe*, not the Army.

He explains why it was not an enemy fighter. 'During the briefing that preceded the sorties, they [the Boston's crew] had, like all the other members of *groupe Lorraine* who took part in this historic session, heard the Wing Intelligence Officer reply to the question of a pilot who asked how protection by friendly fighters would be assured, 'There will be so many allied fighters in the air that you will not see the sky through them.'

This is analogous to the hyperbole in the classic reply of the American bomber pilot who, when asked about the flak on a sortie from which he had just returned, replied, 'You could walk on it'.

Less extravagantly, Eisenhower had declared on the eve of the landings, 'If you see any aeroplanes above you, they will be ours'. He probably called them 'airplanes'.

For the Belgians in the RAF the invasion was a long stride along the route that should soon take them to their homeland. Michel 'Mike' Donnet, who ended the war as a wing commander and served on in his own country's air force to reach the rank of Lieutenant-General, was one of those who had well earned this reward. A Belgian born in England, he was a sergeant pilot in the Belgian Air Force at the outbreak of war. Taken prisoner by the Germans in May, 1940, he was released and, early the next year, found an SV4 trainer aircraft in a hangar near Brussels. He, another pilot, Divoy, and some friends made it serviceable. On 14 July, 1941, wearing uniform, Donnet and Divoy took off, flew to England and joined the RAF.

Immediately on the collapse of France and withdrawal of the British Expeditionary Force, several Belgian pilots had been able to reach England and join the RAF. Twenty-nine of them fought in the Battle of Britain.

The Air Ministry decided to make one flight of 609 (West Riding) Squadron (Auxiliary Air Force) all-Belgian. It was commanded by Flight Lieutenant Jean Offenberg, who, in June, 1941, became the first Belgian to receive the DFC. Among his pilots was Rodolphe de Memricourt de Grunne, who had fourteen victories fighting for Franco in the Spanish Civil War of 1936–1939. (*Oberst* Werner Mölders, who preceded Lieutenant-General Adolf Galland as General of Fighters made the same score in Spain. He shot down 87 more over France and England before being killed in action against the RAF in November, 1941). It must be remembered, however, that the fighters of Franco's air force and the Italians and Germans who fought for him were much superior to those of their opponents.

In April, 1942, the squadron replaced its Spitfires by Typhoons. In March, 1944, it was posted to 123 Wing, 84 Group, 2nd TAF. On 5 June, in company with 198 Squadron, also flying Typhoons, it attacked and destroyed Rommel's Headquarters on the Cherbourg peninsula, but the *Feldmarschall* happened to be absent. On D-Day it was engaged on armed reconnaissance over the invasion area. Among 609's commanders were Manu Geerts, DFC, and Raymond Lallemant, DFC (and bar), known as '*Cheval*'. Another Belgian, Remy Van Lierde, DFC and two bars, commanded 164, which also flew Typhoons.

Another Belgian flight was formed in 131 Squadron. By November, 1941, so many Belgian pilots had arrived in England that, adding them to the nucleus in 131, an all-Belgian squadron, No 350, was formed, with a British C.O. – 131's commander, Squadron Leader J. M. Thompson, DFC (later DSO with a bar to his DFC). He was then credited with eight victories and scored two more over Malta that summer. From April, 1942, 350 Squadron always had a Belgian in command.

Donnet had been commissioned, rose quickly in rank and won a DFC. By March, 1943, he was a squadron leader, in command of 64 Squadron. In November, after twenty-six months with 64, he was rested and sent as an instructor to the Fighter Leaders' School. In April, 1944, he took over 350

Squadron, which joined 135 Wing – led by Wing Commander D. E. Kingaby, DFM and two bars, who had shot down 23 hostiles, in 84 Group the following month.

Contemplating his feelings when the pilots were gathered in discussion after the two-hour briefing on the eve of D-Day, Donnet writes with as much emotion as though he were about to return home immediately, but it is more a retrospective depth of feeling than anticipatory. 'In the words that were exchanged, in the tones of voice, one recognized hope, hatred [of the enemy], love and the will to conquer. I remembered the faces that the words recalled: Jacques, Jean, Henri . . . and which this evening gave rise to a whole range of sentiments that had been hidden until now. I remembered all these faces, of those who were still with us and those who were no longer. Outside night had fallen, black and mysterious, enveloping the wings of our aeroplanes. The propellers turned in a cloud of dust, men were busy but glanced now and then at the sky and the sea, speculating. There was electricity in the air.'

In the morning, the purpose of the extensive night flying the squadron had been practising became apparent on D-Day, when it was selected for dawn and dusk patrols over the beachhead. On the first, which lasted two hours, twelve aircraft took off at 0440 hrs and flew to Le Havre, where they met flak from German ships, which shot down Flight Lieutenant Sus Venesoen, who baled out and came down in the Channel, never to be seen again. On the second, no enemy aircraft were seen; nor were they on the third, between 2200 hrs and midnight.

In October, 1942, the second Belgian squadron, No 349, was formed, to be sent to defend the Belgian Congo. Its destination was changed to Lagos, Nigeria, where it arrived in November that year. Following the defeat of the Germans in North Africa, No 349 returned to England in May, 1943. In March, 1944, under the command of a former member of 609 Squadron, Squadron Leader Ivan Dumonceau de Bergendal, known as 'The Duke' – destined to reach the rank of Major-General in the Belgian Air Force – 349 also joined 135 Wing. At 0830 on 6 June the Wing took off on a patrol of the Normandy beaches during which it attacked two flak ships. It flew five patrols that day, shot down four Ju88s and damaged five. Warrant Officer Van Molkot was shot down and had to bale out over France.

Nowithstanding their country's small size, Belgium's airmen made a handsome contribution to victory throughout the war.

Whatever their nationality and whether in fighters or bombers, the pilots and other air crew who operated over the invasion area that first day all viewed the same awesome spectacle. Those who had taken off in the dark saw bombs exploding along the French shore and immediate hinterland, the red glow of fires spreading, multi-coloured tracer from light flak flickering and darting in long, curving, interweaving streaks, great crimson daubs pocking the sky where heavy flak exploded. Those who flew at the lower levels could see the phosphorescent wake of ships and boats forging towards the enemy-held shore: 2,727 of them crossed the Channel that day.

When the sun rose at H-Hour, 0530, they saw tanks crawling out of the big landing ships and men swarming down the ramps at the bows of the smaller landing craft. They saw, and many heard, battleships, cruisers and destroyers bombarding the German positions: the boom of the great guns and the long yellow flames licking out of their muzzles; the thunderous, dazzling detonations when the shells struck, the clouds of dust and débris, the tumbling buildings, the smoke that hung over the battlefield; the charging, stumbling, falling infantrymen lashed by machine guns, shelled by mortars and cannon from concrete emplacements among the sandhills.

Some witnessed from the air one of the most demented examples ever recorded of brave but unthinking, wastefully self-sacrificing compliance with orders. One of the surprises to be sprung on the enemy was the invention of the 'swimming tank': conventional tanks made amphibious by fitting them with a propeller and buoyant waterproof canvas skirt. This ingenious transformation was valid only over a short distance and in calm water. One landing ship launched its tanks further from the beach and into a rougher sea than intended. When the first tank quickly sank, it was a tragedy. When those that immediately followed also went down, tragedy degenerated into farce: none of the tank commanders was deterred by the fate of his predecessors. Of the thirty-two that waddled off the bow ramp into the waves, twenty-seven sank. If the spirit of *Maréchal* Bosquet had a heavenly view of events, he must have reiterated his admiring but deprecatory comment on the charge of the Light Brigade ninety years earlier: '*C'est magnifique, mais ce n'est pas la guerre*'.

8

BUILDING AIRFIELDS AND
SERVICING AIRCRAFT
UNDER FIRE

No 3205 Servicing Commando Unit, RAF sailed from Gosport at 1100 on D-Day aboard four LCTs. It comprised five officers, 176 other ranks, twenty three-ton lorries, two 350 gallon water tenders, two fifteen-hundredweight trucks, a jeep and four motorcycles.

The unit began to disembark at 0800 on D+1. In the naval crews' hurry to unload and return to England, the doors of one LCT were opened prematurely and two three-tonners were driven off into deep water. Both vehicles and the equipment they carried were lost, but the occupants swam ashore. Two airmen were injured when a land mine on the beach blew up their lorry.

No 3207 RAF Servicing Commando Unit went aboard two British LCIs and an American LST at Gosport at 1800 on D-Day. Early next morning the convoy was attacked by torpedo bombers. The LCT was hit amidships forward and caught fire. An airman was killed and another badly burned. A motor torpedo boat took some of the survivors off. The remainder assembled on the poop, which presently broke away from the holed and burning hull. Although the poop did not sink, its deck was awash, a cold wet place on which to await rescue – which came in the form of a United States Coastguard cutter. At 0800 on 7 June the unit began to go ashore on Gold beach, between Ver sur Mer and Grave sur Mer.

Nos 3209 and 3210 also landed that day, the former near Beny sur Mer. Alan McQuillin, who was in 3210, recalls that he embarked on an LCT at Gosport at 0900 on the sixth. At 0430 next morning, off the Normandy coast, an LCT ahead was sunk. He landed on Juno beach, near Graye sur Mer, at 0930. His party had become separated from the rest of the unit, so spent several hours that day and the next seeking their comrades, harassed throughout by snipers, air raids and a false gas alarm.

No 3206 followed on 15 June and 3208 on 16. For all four SCUs their first night at the beachhead was noisy and luridly illuminated by courtesy of the German artillery.

This type of unit was created in January, 1942, to service aircraft on airfields close to the battlefield. They comprised tradesmen of every relevant technical branch, as well as cooks and clerks. They had their own transport and carried tents as well as all necessary tools. Everyone had to learn to drive and maintain motor vehicles. The first three to be formed took part in the North African landings on 8 November that year.

The men selected had to be ready to defend themselves from the moment they disembarked. Training by Commando instructors was even more demanding than for seaborne Combined Operations airmen. The syllabus embraced forced marches, battle courses, the use of weapons, unarmed combat, swimming, navigating by compass and map, aircraft recognition and familiarity with anti-aircraft guns. They also went to sea in a landing craft, tank, and practised landings.

By D-Day for Normandy the establishment for an SCU was two officers and 150 other ranks, but in practice this varied up to four officers and from 130 to over 170 ORs.

Originally khaki battledress was worn, but before embarkation for France RAF blue was resumed. Pride of service and the RAF's good-natured pretended disdain for 'squaddies' no doubt made this a popular order. It had the advantage that, when pilots landed to refuel and rearm at a forward airstrip, they were instantly able to identify the men who would do these jobs, from soldiers and members of the RAF Regiment or airfield construction units, who all wore khaki and might be there. It also imposed an unforeseen danger. When work-worn, faded, discoloured by lubricant stains and dust, RAF blue bore an unfortunate resemblance to German field grey. French peasants seeing RAF troops for the first time were wont to shout insults and imprecations at them. Worse, at the sharp end of the fighting, where there was no clear boundary between ground held by allies or enemy, they were sometimes shot at by their own side. SCU personnel who had taken part in a landing were entitled to wear the Combined Operations badge – a hard-earned distinction.

It seems anomalous that among the plethora of prestigious insignia – aircrew, parachutist, commando, SAS, tank crew, submariner et al – the British Army has never so rewarded the one arm without which all the efforts of the others and of all the fighting Services could never have won any war in history; the men who do most of the fighting and ultimately have to take enemy ground and hold it: the infantry. Every foot soldier who has been in action merits a symbol to wear.

Concurrently with the landing of Servicing Commando Units went the preparation of airfields by the RAF's Airfield Construction Branch and the Royal Engineers.

The landing grounds were numbered, those for the RAF prefixed 'B' and those for the USAAF 'A'. They were of three types: emergency landing strip (ELS), six hundred metres long, for aircraft in trouble and unable to reach any other; rearming and refuelling strip (RRS), for aircraft operating from England and unable to return there for these services because of damage, mechanical trouble or lack of petrol, or to save time in order to fly another sortie as soon as possible; advanced landing ground (ALG) capable of accommodating fifty-four fighters, with a runway twelve hundred to seventeen hundred metres long and forty to fifty wide.

There were usually three runways, used in turn according to the amount of traffic and whether affected by dust or rain. Only one or two were of pierced steel plank (PSP) or wire mesh, the ot:.er(s) grass – a euphemism that most often meant bare earth. Some runways were made of PSP, oblong sections with holes in them for lightness, slotted together. Others consisted of squares of steel wire mesh Somerfield track. On all, taxi tracks and dispersal areas were also laid. As the aeroplanes that would use them were not much affected by crosswinds, runways were oriented in the direction of the prevailing wind.

Preparing the ground before laying PSP or mesh needed a vast amount of equipment: bulldozers, scrapers, tractors, carryalls, rollers. If all went well, a runway could be made in two days – and aircraft often used a field before this work had been completed. It took five or six days to make a 1200-metre runway and ten or eleven for one of 1700 metres. The shorter runway needed 2560 rolls of wire mesh, each weighing 250 Kg – in all 640 tonnes – plus 30,000 pegs and clips weighing 100 tonnes: which meant 370 three-ton-lorry loads; and there was space in a lorry for only seven rolls of mesh.

All this work was done under fire from the enemy's versatile 88mm guns that had put up a formidable anti-aircraft barrage throughout the war and ravaged Allied armour in the desert. By D+10 twelve airfields were in use in the British sector and twelve in the American.

Maintenance was as arduous as construction. Wire mesh runways had to be watered at night to keep the dust down. After rain, a leveller was dragged over them by a lorry or tractor to disperse the water and level the surface. PSP had to be lifted, mud removed, ruts filled and the steel plates carefully relaid level.

Corporal T. I. Young was a wireless mechanic in 6175 Servicing Echelon. Its parent unit was 121 Wing of 2nd TAF, which comprised three Typhoon squadrons, Nos 174, 175 and 245.

Ian Young was fortunate in his character. The vicissitudes he underwent from the moment of embarkation for the invasion beaches and during several weeks to come were not the common lot of an airman in his capacity. They must have been no small surprise, yet he describes them with amusing imperturbability.

That sometimes melancholy seventeenth/eighteenth-century philosopher, Thomas Hobbes (who really had little cause to complain, as he lived 91 years), denigrated the sort of existence that one might apply to the first three months in Normandy: 'No arts, no letters, no society; and which is worst of all, continual fear and danger of violent death; and the life of man, solitary, poor, nasty, brutish, and short'. Certainly there was no time for the pursuit of culture or pleasure, but life on a fighter wing was far from solitary. Aircraftmen were not generously paid and the conditions they endured in the battle area were undeniably nasty, though hardly brutish: but the threat of violent death was all too apparent. Happily, life for most was not as short as they might often have expected.

For Corporal Young D-Day meant immediate departure towards the battleground, but his arrival there was later than the immediate urgency suggested. He writes, 'On the morning of 6 June we were wakened by the C.O. broadcasting the news over the Tannoy system that the invasion had started and the Wing would be on the road within two hours. We were warned to take only necessities. Units of 2nd TAF were entirely mobile, everything fitted into vehicles.'

By midday they were on their way to an undisclosed destination, the convoy filtering into roads choked with traffic. The Wing travelled in two parties, 'A' and 'B'. '"A" party disappeared – we learned later that they went by air and landed in Normandy under shell fire.

'I never knew where we went, but we spent some boring days confined to camp and sleeping in cramped bell tents while all the vehicles were waterproofed for a possible wet landing. From time to time we heard of the sad loss of some of our aircraft against invasion targets.'

Until their own ground crews could reach the landing fields being built in Normandy, all fighter and fighter-bomber squadrons were operating from bases in England, where their aeroplanes were serviced by ground crews of Air Defence of Great Britain. From 1919 the RAF had consisted of two Branches: Air Defence of Great Britain and Coastal Area. In 1936 it was reorganized into Bomber, Fighter, Coastal and Training Commands. Reversion to ADGB in 1943 was a temporary measure and the title Fighter Command was resumed after the war. In 1968 Bomber and Fighter were merged in Strike Command.

One morning B Party were roused at two o'clock and the convoy set off towards the south coast in a stream of tank transporters, lorries, jeeps and guns, a thirty-mile journey that took all night. Ian Young 'can't remember which of the ports we used, but it was crammed with LSTs and every sort of craft. We got some sort of breakfast provided by the WRVS.' This admirable organization of indefatigable ladies of all ages had not yet been granted 'Royal' in its title. A story circulated that when a Polish pilot who had made his way to England asked what the initials represented and was informed that they stood for 'Women's Voluntary Service', he beamed in anticipatory delight at the interpretation he mistakenly put on the the type of service available.

'B' party of 121 Wing boarded an LST. The vehicle containing Eric Young's kit was a converted ambulance – 'Hopelessly underpowered,' he recalls. 'The driver was unable to park it to the satisfaction of the loading officer. I was instructed under panic conditions to remove my "small kit" [a haversack containing toilet articles and underclothes] and rejoin my unit as the ship was about to cast off. The vehicle was to come by a later ship. I suppose it is difficult to believe, but I remembered to grab all the important things like bars of soap for barter in occupied France and, of course, my Brylcreem.' This was a jocular allusion to the other Services' burlesque term for the RAF, 'Brylcreem Boys' – a product widely advertised by the depiction of a smiling airman with abundant glossy hair.

'Unfortunately I forgot my rifle and ammunition! I was probably the only serviceman to land in France without a weapon. I felt obliged to tell the Signals Officer, who muttered, "For God's sake don't tell anyone else". He was a decent sort, an amateur like myself.'

That evening the ship dropped anchor off Arromanches. 'We slept on board in dreadful conditions below deck in bunks with about eighteen inches between the layers of bodies. Suddenly alarm bells rang all over the ship and American sailors wearing huge steel helmets ran through our quarters closing watertight doors – we were entombed. We spent an uncomfortable ten minutes listening to the sounds of AA firing and aircraft. A few bombs were dropped, but not near the ship.

'In the morning we found the LST beached with the ramp down and doors open. As my wagon had been left behind, I had to find space in a loaded 15cwt. Going down the ramp I clung to the back step. Diesel oil had accidentally flooded the deck and vehicles were sliding about. Half-way down the ramp the truck struck the side and I fell or jumped off and had to run down after it. Where the ramp met the beach, a deep pool of water had formed. Not only did I create a record by landing without a rifle, but also I was the only member of the unit who had a "wet" landing!'

The convoy wound up the beach along a track cleared of mines. The weather had been dry for several days and dust penetrated vehicles, equipment and clothing. 'A sign with the slogan "Dust means death" did not help. We drove on past 25-pounder field guns at the roadside – these are short-range guns. How much farther are we going? On the ridge about a mile away we saw the smoke of shell bursts and just then a dust-covered jeep came to meet us. It was driven by the SLA [Squadron Leader, Administration] whose dust-covered uniform had a distinctly German appearance. Our officer asked if we had far to go. "Not far," he replied, "make for the shell bursts on the top of the rise".'

They drove into a walled field, the shelling stopped, they dispersed the vehicles and unloaded. 'A' party, who had landed in Dakotas, under fire that destoyed at least one aircraft, were already there. Young dug himself a shallow 'trench' five feet long. The shelling resumed and 'I dropped into the doubtful cover of my six-inch trench. It might have been adequate for our warrant officer, called "Tom Thumb" (but not to his face).

'We were shelled sporadically for days by self-propelled 88mm guns. Wing Commander Green, DFC tried without success to spot them by coming in to land and setting up dust, then opening up and zooming off again, turning to see if he could spot the gun flashes. On occasions the CO, ensconced in Flying Control, would give us a running commentary: "That was an air burst . . . that landed plumb in the middle . . ." and so on. The shells would blow out the pegs holding the Somerfield track and parts of the runway would roll up. The RE did a great job, often under fire, replacing it.

'We were at risk from friendly fire. When some foolhardy German attacked the beaches, so much anti-aircraft fire went up that bits and pieces showered down. When I heard metal "ping" on the cookhouse tins one afternoon, I took cover under a wagon.'

He and another airman dug a hole two and a half feet deep, made an arched roof over it with runway track and covered this with tarpaulin and six inches of earth. They were 'very snug' for two or three nights, then a battery of 5.9 guns arrived just across the road and would open fire at any time, day or night. 'The concussion was appalling and earth rained down on us in our shelter.' They lost it soon after, when the Medical Officer made an inspection and condemned it. 'We never thought of the consequences had there been heavy rain.'

The enemy shelling ceased, the Typhoons returned to England to be fitted with dust filters and 'we had an easy time' by comparison with the first days ashore. 'Occasionally a brave but foolish German would shoot up the airfield, doubtless he would not survive. One day working in the test vehicle I heard the Bofors guns and saw tracer passing between our section and the cookhouse vehicles – another quick dive under the truck!'

Corporal Ian Young's wry reminiscences reflect the typical humourous stoicism of the RAF's ground crews, who not only worked in frequently dangerous conditions and sometimes saw their comrades killed or wounded, but were also armed and ready to defend their airfields.

In all areas of France there were many people who detested the British, disaffected by the retreat of the British Expeditionary

Force in 1940 and blaming this for the routing of their own army and air force. Some even fostered a lingering, irrational resentment for the laying waste of thousands of square miles of northern France in the First World War, in which their own artillery and bomber aeroplanes had done no less damage than their Allies. More reasonably, there was no doubt offence taken at the bastard children whom any invading or conquering force leaves behind. Allied aircrew who had been shot down and were trying to evade capture were in danger from such folk, but their antagonism waned after the invasion. Even after the landings, however, some remained actively aggressive in the coastal areas.

It was not only Germans snipers who menaced the invaders during the early days of the landings. The number of Frenchmen and women who collaborated with the Germans formed only a small part of the population, but amounted to thousands. Some traitors acted only as informers, betraying members of the Resistance and Allied pilots or other air crew who had been shot down and were trying to make their way back to Britain. Others played an active part as *francs tireurs* and *franches tireuses*. Many Frenchwomen cohabited with Germans of all ranks, others even married them and were allowed to live on the coast in places from which honest patriots had been driven out or excluded.

On one of the newly made landing fields around which the RAF Regiment was dealing with snipers, the troops had shot two women who were armed with rifles. A third was shooting from the top of a church tower. There was no cover for anyone to approach, so a field gun had to bring her vantage point crashing down, and her flattened remains with it.

An RAF Intelligence officer who saw half a dozen *Wehrmacht* troops' bodies soon after they had been killed in a fire fight was shown a photograph found on one of them. It was of a dummy haystack in which eight men and women of the Resistance had been caught and shot by German soldiers. The corpses lay outside it, four German soldiers stood grinning down at them. By their side was the civilian Frenchman with a shotgun who had betrayed them. The photograph was sent at once to the appropriate authorities, who would soon enough trace the traitor and make him pay for his crime with his life. Meanwhile there were British airmen going about their duties on the airstrips while snipers of both sexes, in and out of uniform, were still free to fire on them.

9

THE FIRST WEEK AND A
GLANCE AT THE FUTURE

The first day had ended. The Typhoons and Spitfires, flying from their home bases, were terrorizing the enemy. The indispensable ancillaries – control, radar, servicing and airfield construction units – were unloading or preparing to go ashore on the morrow.

Each of the five beaches had its own Air Staff aboard a Headquarters ship, under whose orders there was a Fighter Direction Tender. Dusk found 83 Group Control Centre ashore and starting to take over from its FDT. The USAAF Control Centre was also in business. Coningham praised them in a despatch, in which he said that they formed effective parts of a single machine, thanks to excellent teamwork between their commanders.

Taken by surprise over the landing area, on the first morning the enemy sent an armoured division racing to the beachhead. The German Generals learned what had been proved in the deserts of North Africa and the mountains of Italy – that it was folly to order large-scale movements by day. Five tanks and 214 self-propelled guns and various types of wheeled and half-tracked vehicles were destroyed.

On D-plus-one Ju88s without fighter escort optimistically cruised over the beachhead and lost twelve of their number before sundown. The next day brought enemy fighters to the beaches to strafe, an intrusion that cost them twenty losses. By night Mosquitos were shooting down bombers. Trade increased after the first couple of days when ninety He177s and 45 Do217s were transferred from Italy and the south of France.

During that day low cloud prevented the heavy bombers working. The Typhoon squadrons of 83 Group were given the area bounded by Caen, Mezidon, Falaise and Villiers-Bocage as their hunting ground. Those of 84 Group were allotted the area east of the beaches as far as a line running from Pont-Audemer through Louviers to Evreux. To give them the range, they carried an auxiliary fuel tank and only four rockets. The Mustang squadrons operated as far south as the line Dreux-Argentan-Flers.

On D-plus-one 345 Squadron met heavy flak at Valoges. Sergeant Autret's aircraft was hit and descended slowly, switch-backing, evidently trying to find a meadow on which to land, until it hit the ground and blew up. Autret made no radio call, so it was presumed that he had been badly wounded. On the same day Sergeant-Major Bonjean, wing man to Captain Perdri-zet, reported that his engine was misbehaving, a few minutes after the leader, Major Accart, had given the order to go over from supplementary to main tank. The aircraft lost height, made erratic short climbs and dives, then plunged into the water. Lieutenant Harmel, who had accompanied Bonjean, saw a boat heading for the place where the Spitfire had made a last gentle dive. He flew at wavetop height but saw only a yellow stain that must have been made by the dye from the dinghy.

The pilots were, like all the other French fighter pilots who flew over their country, eager to land there. Colonel Jean Gisclon served in *Groupe 2/5 La Fayette*, flew 300 operational sorties, scored five victories, accumulated 6000 flying hours and retired from the French Air Force in 1960, with many decorations. He writes: 'Despite their longing, the disciplined pilots awaited the order'. Before it came, Sergeant-Major Cartier and his No 2, Lieutenant Longeville, ran short of petrol and lobbed in at a Normandy strip. The only people they met were Americans and the only souvenir they brought back was a flower, which was immediately preserved in a perspex frame.

The RAF saw about sixty enemy aircraft, of which they

destroyed eleven Ju88s and a FW190. At 1000 hrs, 126 (Spitfire) Wing engaged twelve Ju88 torpedo bombers and a He177 carrying radio-controlled bombs that were about to attack the ships lying off the beach. Eight Ju88s were shot down and one probable was also claimed.

At 1600 three Typhoon squadrons, 182, 245 and 247, were sent to back up 61 Brigade and 41 Commando, which were having difficulty in capturing Port-en-Bessin. Eight aircraft attacked a site where artillery was well dug in, while fifteen others smashed the pillboxes that surrounded the area. This enabled the troops to take the port and join up with the Americans on their flank at Omaha beach.

The cloud base was only about 1000 ft, which made the fighter bombers highly vulnerable to light flak; it shot down fifteen Typhoons and ten Mustangs. Forty more sustained varying amounts of damage. Typhoons flew 493 sorties and Mustangs 259 that day. Reconnaissance Spitfires flew 245 sorties during which two were shot down. Throughout the night, Mosquitos, Mitchells and Bostons dropped flares over the roads to illuminate the enemy's troop movements while his tanks rumbled towards the front.

So the air operations continued day and night on the same scale.

Lieutenant-General Galland, *Luftwaffe* Chief of Fighters, wrote of this hard time, 'Our pilots were waging a real jungle warfare. Wherever a fighter aircraft rolled out of its camouflaged lair, an enemy immediately pounced on it. The danger of being detected and destroyed by the enemy was ever present. At last we retired into the forests. Before and after each sortie the aircraft were rolled in and out of their leafy protection with great difficulties and much damage. Soon the Allies applied carpet bombing to those parts of the forests suspected of hiding German fighter aircraft. Those squadrons that did not perform masterpieces of camouflage and improvisation, and had had a good run of luck into the bargain, were beaten up in no time.

'Fourteen days after the invasion the units had sunk so low in their fighting strength that neither by driving the personnel nor

by material replacements could they be put on their feet again.'
An odd expression by which to refer to aerial activity. Perhaps
he had Hermes's winged sandals in mind.

By D-plus-seven 532 Allied aircraft had been lost, mostly to
flak, on 49,000 sorties. By-D-plus 31, they flew 158,000 sorties,
during which flak and fighters had shot down 1,284 aircraft.

The airfield construction squadrons and Royal Engineers had
three landing grounds ready on D-plus-two. B1, at Asnelles,
was an emergency landing strip; B2, Bazenville, rearming and
refuelling strip; B3, Croix sur Mer, rearming and refuelling
strip. The last-named was the first ready to receive aircraft.

Early that morning, 8 June, Wing Commander Johnny Johnson was given the news and asked to 'send over a couple of good
pilots as soon as possible to see if the strip was fully operational
and whether the ground crews were organized to cope with
rapid refuelling and rearmament'. The squadron commander
and his wing man whom he sent returned soon to confirm that
'all was well'.

Presently he led 144 Wing on a sweep, after which they landed
at St Croix. Twenty minutes later the Spitfires were ready to fly
again. But before taking off on a second patrol and returning to
Ford in Sussex there was time to examine the strange surround-
ings. His account of the brief halt at B3 gives a disarmingly
detached impression of the duality with which a seasoned
campaigner regards the facets of warfare: the serious business for
which they are there and such recreation and comfort as can be
snatched at odd moments off duty.

There was an orchard nearby, in which a mobile operations
room had been set up. Dead Germans lay around, 'where they
had fallen in this pleasant glade'. Villagers in St Croix had seen
the Spits land, and, as this was a special event, they turned up
bearing fruit, wine and flowers, unconcerned about the shells
that now and then burst in the surrounding fields. The Wing
Commander noticed several coveys of partridge running around
and was glad that he had included a shotgun in his baggage
when packing the caravan in which he slept, which would soon
be crossing to France. He watched 'the unending stream of

vehicles', trucks, tanks, armoured cars, moving from the landing ships towards the front line. The 'incalculable value of our complete air superiority was clearly demonstrated to me'. After a 'leisurely snack' they were in the air again. A few days later the whole wing was established at B3.

Meanwhile, three nights after its exacting task on the late eve and in the early hours of D-Day, 617 Squadron was chosen for another prestigious operation. Dr Barnes Wallace, who had designed the bouncing bomb used on the dams raid, had invented a new conventional bomb that weighed 12,000lb, the Tallboy. It not only had great penetrating capacity but also cataclysmic explosive force, which displaced a million cubic feet of earth and left a crater that needed 5,000 tons of soil to fill.

Nineteen of Cheshire's Lancasters were to carry this annihilating monster, accompanied by four Lancesters of 83 Squadron with target flares and 1,000lb bombs. The targets were a bridge carrying the main line between south-west France and the Normandy battle zones and a long tunnel near Saumur.

The 83 Squadron aircraft were to mark the targets and destroy the bridge. Their radar equipment did not perform up to scratch, the flares went wide and the bridge was undamaged. Cheshire himself marked the farther end of the tunnel, but the immense clouds of smoke from each Tallboy temporarily blotted out his flares, which caused much delay. One was dropped on the tunnel roof and several were dropped in the cutting leading to it, which accomplished the purpose of the raid. That stretch of line remained unusable until the Germans had been driven out of the region.

10

GERMAN TORPEDO AIRCRAFT
ATTACK INVASION SHIPS

In narratives about the air war little recognition has been given
to the German torpedo units. The importance of the aerial
torpedo as a weapon against the invasion fleet has been obscured
by the coverage given to bomber and fighter operations, both
offensive and defensive, over land during the Normandy
fighting.

Torpedo attacks from the air against Allied shipping in the
Channel and lying off the Normandy coast from D-Day had a
usefulness that was at least as great as that of the bombing and
strafing of factories, troops, tanks, vehicles and all the other
obvious targets of non-maritime aircraft. The archive of III/KG
26, No III *Gruppe* of Kampfgeschwader 26 LT (*Luft Torpedo*)
explains why.

The exposition, or diatribe, begins forthrightly. 'By speech
and written word we had been told that when the invasion began
the war would be fought in the decisive stadium [It was, of
course, the fighting, not the arena, that was decisive]. The
beginning of the invasion had been awaited for months, yet
when it happened the torpedo units operated with the most out-
dated equipment. That we did not have better aircraft was a
consequence of the bombing campaign. However, it was incomprehensible that we had to fight the most decisive campaign
with old-fashioned tools.

'It had long been known that the aerial torpedo is the best
weapon to use against ships. The enemy could, because of his

air supremacy, strike at our key industries and road and rail transportation systems and vehicles. We were unable to attack the enemy's key industries. But the enemy could make use of his key industries only when they were delivered to the battle area. Thus, for us, the enemy's key industries were his supply ships. The shipping fleet was a concentration of key industry. It was attackable by us. Only there could the enemy be grievously hit.

'Also, for attacking ships, only the best equipment is good enough. The enemy knew where his weak point lay. We could not take much effective action against it, however good our crews.'

To launch a torpedo accurately from the air needed great skill and, usually, courage in the face of gunfire. The German aerial torpedo had a range of 2,900 yards and a speed of forty kilometres an hour. It had to be dropped from a height of between forty and sixty metres, into water with a minimum depth of thirty metres. The maximum acceptable wind strength was forty kilometres an hour.

D-Day found torpedo *Geschwader* II K6 26(LT) dispersed between north Germany and the south of France. *Gruppe* I was in Grove, not yet operational, still being equipped. *Gruppe* II was divided between Grossenbrode and Eichwalde with nearly forty serviceable aircraft. *Gruppe* III was in Montpellier and operationally ready. *Gruppe* IV was at Lübeck-Blankenzee, fully functioning as a training unit. Early on the morning of 6 June, No II was ordered to move to Valence, in the Rhône valley. For tactical reasons, its No 6 Staffel was to be based at Montélimar.

Immediately on the landings in Normandy, the 3rd Air Fleet ordered all available aircraft to take part in the defence, which brought the torpedo units, flying the JU88, into the operational area. Until the arrival of No II *Gruppe*, only No III was in a position to operate there.

Gruppe III was not given a daylight task. Its commander managed to persuade the air fleet commander that his crews could not reach the beachhead and deliver an attack before dusk. From Montpellier to the coast between Cherbourg and Le Havre was 900 kilometres, so a refuelling stop was necessary at Rennes or Cognac on the way back.

At midday twenty-five aircraft of No III took off and, in view of the Allies' total air supremacy, were ordered to fly at 200 metres altitude. By way of Tours and Rennes and the Cherbourg cape they arrived over the target area at dusk. As soon as they were over land they were attacked by fighters. They could evade these attacks only by flying low over trees and hedges. But the real shock came in the target area. Such a huge number of ships had been assembled, with massive firepower, as had never been seen. The closely ranked fleet comprising vessels of all kinds made it impossible for anyone to start a torpedo attack. No approach to, or way through, this mass of shipping could be contrived. Wherever the Ju88s went in the Seine Bay the crowded anchorage was impenetrable. Finally they had to try elsewhere, looking for a chance to make an attack in the area between Seine Bay and the English coast.

Rudy Schmidt writes, 'That evenng the English Channel swarmed with ships! All of them had very strong defensive armament [This was not true of all ships or even most. Small ships were lightly armed,] and many had barrage balloons tethered to them. The aircraft crews could not recognize most of them as they looked down through cloud. Only by chance could one see these shapeless, grey forms when they emerged from the murk. Above 300 metres enemy night fighters abounded. So the torpedo pilots went down as low as possible, hunting for a solitary target. Then finally they made some attacks but scored no hits.

'On the flight home via Rennes and also as we were coming in to land at base, we had contact with night fighters. Nearly all the time we had the sawing noise of enemy radar equipment in our ears. As soon as it grew louder one knew that 'he' was directly behind and in the blink of an eye the gun button might be pressed. The only chance of surviving was to keep a sharp lookout astern and make a hard turn to the right. On account of the night fighters the runway lights were lit sporadically. Always when an aircraft was heard so low over the airfield that it was obviously about to land, the lights came on briefly. Corrections of course could be made only by the approach lighting. For this brief moment the night fighters waited.

'After our tanks had been filled we would start again – blind! That was better than having a night fighter on your neck during your take-off run.

'In the greyness of morning our machines came back to base. We are weary and breathless.

'On the same day, at noon, we were briefed for another operation. The Commanding Officer set a different course. To evade the fighters, we went via the Gironde estuary, out to sea and kept away from the land so as not to be picked up by radar. The flight was uneventful, but in the target area the same experience as on the day before awaited us. We sank no ships and were shot at by warships. Again we suffered damage to aircraft and serious injuries to crews. The defences were even stronger.'

The *Gruppe* was prepared for a night operation over the invasion area. The officers were told that many factors were going to be different henceforth. The experience of the past thirteen months would, however, be important. In particular the enemy's defences had completely changed. They were stronger and more concentrated, there was more fighter cover over the target area and above all the positioning of the radar units and the early warning of enemy [German] aircraft were grave matters. Also the British agents in Occupied France played an exceptional part.

Major Ernst Thomsen, the Commanding Officer, intended to fly on that day's operation. In view of the way matters had gone on the previous day, he chose a different route to the coast, hoping to avoid the enemy fighters that barred the way. Aircraft were to take off at ten-minute intervals and he wanted to be in the target area by moonrise.

The change of route proved a good idea, for none of the aircraft that returned had met enemy fighters before reaching the target area. The situation in the combat zone had hardly changed and was soon to grow more difficult. In contradiction of the information given before taking off, more barrage balloons were seen. The crews reported stronger defences around the big ships that were presumably carrying troops. They could scarcely get near them. They also saw hospital ships with their lights on, lying in Seine Bay.

As soon as *Gruppe* II had arrived in the south of France it flew a few sorties over the Mediterranean in expectation of an imminent Allied landing there by forces based in Italy. It was to be a long wait. The invasion did not come until 15 August.

No II had forty serviceable aircraft and as many crews. Major Teske, its commander, had waited for No III to gain some experience to pass on before beginning operations over the Channel. His crews were now ready to start. He ordered an even more easterly course to the coast.

No III put up fourteen aircraft that evening. Its attack area lay off the French coast. No II's area was off the English coast, where ships passed on their way from the Isle of Wight direct to the Seine estuary.

Major Teske's account of his and his other crews' experiences that night is as follows, 'When darkness fell we took off at fifteen-minute intervals, so that we would not be in one another's way over the target area. Our route was via Dijon and Reims to the mouth of the Somme. Between Lyon and Paris we were fired at by a night fighter, but luckily were not hit. We dived steeply at once and levelled out almost brushing the ground. After a short while I gained a little height because it is not safe to fly very low at night over strange country. We flew at 100 metres for the rest of the way. When we reached the coast we were able to go lower, hoping to attack a large ship.

'Fifteen minutes later we were in the middle of the invasion area. In front of us and on both sides were warships of all kinds and sizes. Naturally we were not unseen. Heavy fire from weapons of all calibres was aimed at us. We made out a large steamer, a freighter with a balloon attached to it. It was on our

9. "Corporal T.I. Young was a wireless mechanic in 6175 Servicing Echelon" (p.64).

10. 137 Typhoon Squadron at Manston, Kent, May, 1944 (see p.103).

11. "Des Davies, a flight mechanic (engines) in 1944" (p.104).

12. Des Davies at the Normandy Veterans' Association Ceremony, Birkenhead, April, 1991.

13. Geoffrey Merriman (see p.111) is second from the right in the middle row of this squad of recruits photographed in September, 1941.

14. "R.E.G. Sheward...
was one of several Britons
resident in Argentina who
returned to England... to
volunteer for the RAF"
(p.131).

15. 263 Squadron, 146 Wing, 84 Group, Antwerp, November, 1944
(see p.131). Sheward is third from the right in the front row.

16. "Pilot Officer John Shellard was also a pilot in 263 Squadron" (p.135).

17. 21 March, 1945. Pilot Officer J.W. Shellard about to take off in RB232 HE-O for an attack on petrol and oil dumps near Deventer in Holland.

starboard at an angle of about seventy degrees and a range of 2,000 metres. An attack with one torpedo to start with – we did not want to fire both. Our height was forty metres and we aimed amidships. Immediately after launching the torpedoes we dived and flew past the ship's stern. We hoped that there were fewer guns on the other side, but we were followed by heavy fire. Beyond there was little space in the crowded anchorage. We could not see another ship in our direct line of fire. We had started the stop watch at the moment of launching the torpedo. It should hit in another minute or so. The time was not yet up when fire should break out in the ship.

'There was nothing more for us here. We had to extricate ourselves from the tumult. But on the intercom the wireless operator announced that a huge flame had erupted [from the ship they had attacked]. Further west we sought another chance to fire our second torpedo. We soon had another ship in sight. We were close to the shore, where the gunfire would be even heavier. We did not approach the ship; the anti-aircraft fire was so intense that we had to break off.

'There was little sense in trying to find another target around here, so deep were we in the beachhead zone and so strong was the defensive fire. We therefore turned north-west towards England.

'We hoped to find a ship on its own, not too heavily armed, in mid-Channel. The visibility was not such that we could fly safely past enemy aircraft, and we would surely some time or other spot a ship ahead. Near the English coast we came upon a long line of merchant ships and naval vessels steering a course for France. Perhaps we could make an attack along the moon-path. We positioned ourselves at a distance and considered how to make the best attack. We had not failed to notice that at least we were not being fired at. Annoyingly, a cloud drifted over the moonpath and obscured our view. When our line of attack cleared, we must be half way along it. We were there already. Flak was fired at us from all sides. The point at which we must fire the torpedo was clear but we could not see the ship well enough to identify. A proper attack was not possible. We left this lot as fast as we could and went to look elsewhere for something to go for.

'We would have to return to the Seine estuary if we were to find another ship. On the way we saw a freighter with two large warships ahead of it. They must be cruisers. We had not definitely identified them, so we did not go near them. We therefore changed our target to the ship next ahead of us. The range was so short that there was no time for careful preparation of the attack. We could see only that it was turning to port. We went past the ship's bows, pressed low over the water and came so close to one of the cruisers that we could see the guns. It had also seen us and had us fully in its sights. We were hit twice, then another in the cockpit. Luckily there were no splinters and no wounds, only a strong rush of air through the cockpit. We set course to return the way we came and found no more damage. To avoid any further risks we stayed low. It was galling that we had not come across another convoy of ships.

'So long as we flew low and over the sea, we met no night fighters. But near the coast if one had to go higher than 300 metres, they were there. With their airborne radar they scanned the air. We heard the apparatus in our earphones, it was a sawing noise. We knew that the louder it was the closer they were. On the approach to the airfield it was the same. Hubert, the wireless operator, saw him first. He fired his twin guns at once and thought that he had got him. At least there was one gone. When we drew near the airfield we received a recognition signal. On our response the lights went on briefly so that we could check our course. Then the place was dark again. We made a circuit and prepared to land. Immediately before we touched down the lights came on and went out as soon as we were on the ground. Nothing was easier meat for a night fighter than an aeroplane while landing.

'Twenty-six aircraft [of No II *Gruppe*] had taken off. Three had been shot at by night fighters when approaching the target area and had to abandon their sorties. Sixteen returned via Cognac. Another had also had to land and arrived back next day. On this operation six aircraft were lost.'

★

III/KG 26's *Kommandeur*, a Doctor of Philosophy, had a distinguished and varied career in two Services and retired as a naval post-captain. He was the *Gruppe's* first commander when it was formed in 1942, but was severely wounded a year later. He commanded it again throughout June, July and August, 1944. He tells us that initially, after the landings, his unit flew over the invasion area at dawn and dusk, but encounters with fighters at those times of day compelled it to resort to night attacks.

He describes a sortie on which he took off at 2200 and flew via Brest to the Bordeaux area. There was four-tenths cloud, its base at 800 metres. Visibility was good, with moonlight. To start with, the crew saw a group of vessels that consisted mostly of warships – torpedo boats, destroyers, escort ships, patrol boats. There was nothing to reward an attack there; they wanted cargo vessels bringing supplies and reinforcements. They flew low, seeking suitable prey, each member of the crew searching his allotted sector, pilot and navigator keeping their eyes on the area ahead, the mechanic to port and starboard, the wireless operator astern. 'A hellish burst of flak broke out as though someone had been waiting for us.' In an instant they were in the midst of it. They were being shot at from all sides. Clouds were scattered around them and, 'worst of all, the red tracer that surrounded us. We were in no position to make an attack.'

His navigator and wireless operator directed him out of the web of bullets and shells. 'We had often experienced the same concentrated fire in places where it was liberally dished out and today we got away with it once more. We had had luck but also much worry.' That they had not been shot down, they attributed to flying so low. It needed the pilot's utmost concentration not to dip a wingtip into the sea when turning, but had the advantage that most of the 'sparkling red beads' flashed past overhead. His wireless operator, Medrow, who took everything in his stride, exclaimed, 'Fellows, it was so thick, we could have landed on it'. Thomsen comments, 'We laughed heartily. It's great when one doesn't lose one's sense of humour.'

They looked elsewhere, in good visibility thanks to the moon.

The water shone like silver. Ahead and to the left a freighter came in sight, but it was too small to bother about. Hardly had they continued their way when a bigger ship lay across their course. She saw them and fired at them with all her guns. Still 500 metres away, Thomsen zoomed above the level at which the fire was aimed. The navigator again gave him the target's estimated speed and position. He fired both torpedoes, then turned to go astern of the ship instead of flying over her. The hand of the stop watch raced round the dial. On the far side of the ship the aircraft came under fire once more. Two or three times a shell passed so close that the crew almost ducked. In front of them they saw more gunfire. They had to get out of this situation. They tried to go lower. So far things had not gone well.

Whichever way they turned, they were trapped in a ring of guns and could not see what had happened to the ship they had attacked. Considering the range at which they had fired the torpedoes and the relative positions of aircraft and target, they were sure they could not have missed. They scooted out of the seething gunfire and set course for Cognac to refuel.

They crossed the coast at 200 metres and found the cloud was even denser than before. There was noticeable interference on the intercom. Thomsen asked his wireless operator if it was caused by another transmitter. It was not. He changed course and kept doing so for ten minutes, but the noise remained in his earphones. They should soon be over Cognac. Tracer spurted at them from a night fighter. Thomsen tried to take evasive action but neither the rudder nor elevators responded. The night fighter fired again, so Thomsen did an aileron turn and by using the throttle obtained some control, but it was not possible to steer properly. If he had indeed sunk the British freighter, then he had got his deserved come-uppance by courtesy of the Royal Air Force.

He did not want to make a crash landing by night. They had been well shot up – the floor hatch blown out and the engine not sounding healthy, the tail unit badly damaged. He asked the navigator where they were and was shown a point on the chart about fifteen kilometres north of Cognac. He told the crew to bale out. When they had done so, he found he could not leave his seat, as his parachute pack was stuck fast. After a struggle he managed to free it and jumped. He landed in a tree and was able to slither down to the ground. He heard a dog barking and five men appeared. When he identified himself their response was hardly welcome: 'We are *Maquis*.' He drew his pistol and pointed it at the man who was apparently the leader. Nobody tried to take his pistol away, and evidently these men were not armed. It turned out that he had come down near Limoges, in one of the strongest Resistance areas, where German troops moved only in armoured vehicles. The leader of these five was 'the Mayor', but there is no mention of the place where this treacherous Frenchman held office. He took the German pilot home, where his wife made coffee and gave him a bed for the night.

'So it came about that I got back to my *Gruppe* before my crew.'

Traditionally, the Germans and French take such a poor view of each other that it would perhaps not have been much gratification to Thomsen, or any other enemy airman who had the living daylights scared out of him, to know that it was Pierre Corneille, in the Seventeenth Century, who wrote encouragingly, 'To win without risk is to triumph without glory'. Not that the *Luftwaffe* did win.

Between D-Day and 1 August the Germans sank eight cruisers, twenty-four destroyers, five MTBs or ML,s, twenty cargo and passenger ships and landing ships. In addition they probably sank three cruisers, five destroyers, three MTBs or MLs, and several landing craft. They damaged two battleships, ten cruisers, eight MTBs or MLs, thirty-one transport and landing ships.

KG 26 LT was responsible for a large part of all this.

11

THE *LUFTWAFFE*: PRELUDE, INVASION, AFTERMATH

Among the great commanders of air forces *Generalleutnant* Adolf Galland stands high in all respects – intelligence, ability, bravery, moral courage (he always defied Göring's bullying) and as a fighter pilot. Although promoted to command the *Luftwaffe's* Fighter Arm at the age of twenty-nine, in November, 1941, he was not the youngest to hold that post; his close friend and immediate predecessor, Werner Mölders, killed in a flying accident, was a year younger. They were rivals in the same competitive way that friendly sportsmen are, with no ill-feeling or jealousy but a determination to excel over each other. The contest between them was about victories in battle. Mölders started the war with the advantage of having destroyed fourteen enemy aircraft in the Spanish Civil War. Galland had also fought in Spain, but scored no kills. His aircraft was a Heinkel 51 biplane and his work was limited to ground strafing, whereas Mölders flew a Me109 and originated the finger four formation. In the first two years of the war Mölders was the more successful and downed his hundredth victim before Galland, but added only one more to his tally before his fatal crash.

'Dolfo' Galland does, however, have a unique distinction; as a Lieutenant-General and still commanding the German fighter force, he kept his rank when he stepped down in authority to become Commanding Officer of a jet fighter (Me262) *Staffel* (squadron) in January, 1945, and led it until 26 April, when he made a forced landing and ended the war in a foxhole with grenade splinters in one leg.

He had begun the war as an *Oberleutant* in command of a Me109E *Staffel* and by its end was credited with 104 victories. All these were against the RAF and USAAF, none was achieved by shooting down Russian aircraft, whose performance, armament and pilots were mostly inferior, nor was his total, like some of his comrades', inflated by successes in the Spanish Civil War, when the same poor quality of the enemy applied.

About the Normandy landings he writes, 'The High Command started from the correct assumption that the invasion had to be repulsed immediately or at least within ten days. If this were not possible the invasion had to be regarded as a *fait accompli*. The immediate urgency was to get the forces in time to their action stations. However, this demanded a knowledge of the time and place of the landing. During the last weeks and months the forces in the west were often alerted in vain. From the point of view of weather and tide conditions the probable date for the landing would be the end of May. The OKW (High Command of the Armed Forces) suspected that the landing would be staged between Dieppe and Dunkirk, or possibly the Seine estuary. The Allied disguise of their intentions by transmitting misleading signals did not remain without effect. Sufficient and effective air reconnaissance over the Channel and the embarkation ports was impossible because of the air superiority of the enemy. The German Command actually groped in the dark until the moment of the landing and even for some time after.'

The code message for action stations was 'Threatening Danger West'. Upon its receipt all units operating in defence of Germany, with the exception of two *Gruppen* of all-weather fighters and two of Me110 'destroyers', were to be thrown into the invasion sector. For this purpose fifty per cent of all units were to be kept in readiness to support the Army as fighter-bombers in low-level attacks. In the event of dire emergency all fighters were to be devoted fully to the land fighting.

On the evening of 5 June the Germans became aware, by monitoring British radio traffic, that preparations for an imminent invasion were in hand. The C-in-C West's evaluation was still that the main invasion would be made elsewhere than seemed apparent and the first wave would be a feint. 'In this way a lot of time was wasted and the issue of the "cue words" was delayed.'

Finally, the *Luftwaffe* acted on its own initiative and started regrouping its forces. 'This was the delayed opening move to the bitterest fighting phase in its history.'

Facing the huge advantage in air strength that the Allies enjoyed, in both defensive cover and attacking power, the Germans' resources were puny. The relevant formations were the 3rd Air Fleet with 2nd, 9th and 10th Flying Corps, the 2nd Air Division, 2nd Fighter Corps and 122 Reconnaissance Group. On the eve of D-Day the Battle Order showed a fighting strength of 481 aircraft, 64 of them reconnaissance, 90 bomber and 100 fighter. At dawn next day 319 of these were available, outnumbered twenty to one by the Allies.

The German ground forces now asked themselves, 'Where is our air force?', as the British Expeditionary Force had wondered four years ago during the retreat from Dunkirk.

The answer in 1940 had been that few fighters were seen over the port while it was being so heavily bombed because, in order to be effective, fighters had to intercept the enemy many miles away. The Army and Navy were not taught that bombers did not drop their loads when directly overhead, but when still some distance from the target; bombs did not fall straight, the speed of the aircraft gave them a forward impetus that curved downwards during their trajectory. When the defeated BEF arrived back in Britain, ignorance and resentment among the khaki rank and file led to numerous occasions of airmen suffering 'grievous bodily harm' from the fists and boots of soldiers on whom they chanced in the street or a pub. Most often the victims were ground tradesmen and had not even been in France.

This time the answer was that the High Command's delay in sending out the executive signal meant that, as Galland puts it, 'preparatory measures could not start early enough'. OKL (High Command Air) did not order the transfer of virtually the whole German fighter force in Germany to France until the day after the invasion began. In consequence the 3rd Air Fleet, which was already based in France, could put up only eighty serviceable fighters of the 2nd and 26th Fighter *Gruppen*. Communications had been so badly disrupted by bombing in the weeks leading up to the invasion that the Commanding General of 2nd Flying Corps at Compiègne did not hear that it had started until 0800 on D-Day.

On 7 and 8 June the movement of the fighters that had been kept in Germany for the country's defence, and all the reserves, a total of some 600, was thrown into disorder before the first of them had taken off. Airfields in France had been allotted and provisioned, but the continuing air raids against them forced last-minute changes of destination. Many of the designated bases had to be abandoned and alternatives improvised. Most of the pilots were used to permanent airfields, lavishly equipped with all facilities and comforts, both technical and domestic. The *Luftwaffe* was the favoured force and Officers' Messes were luxurious. Among the architectural details were grab handles on each side of every urinal stall, so that the officers who had drunk too much during the frequent manly Teutonic revelry could vomit without reeling about or falling over and cracking their square skulls. The hard lying and generally primitive way of life on hastily extemporized air strips unsettled many of these young gentlemen. To aggravate their discomfort, the hastily prepared fields had little or no camouflage and were readily found by the Allied bombers and ground-attack fighters.

The long foreseen, carefully planned displacement was not the smoothly executed process that had been taken for granted. Instead, it degenerated into turmoil and suffered heavy losses of which not all were caused by direct enemy action.

Earlier in the year General Galland had reported to the RLM (State Ministry of Aviation); 'Between January and April our daytime fighters lost over 1,000 pilots'. The huge majority, of course, were brought down by RAF or USAAF fighters and air gunners in day bombers, but some were also lost to the usual accidents. The German fighter pilot strength had shrunk so much that the flying schools were having to hurry reinforcements through their courses.

The same blight that had affected the RAF during the Battle of Britain now hit the *Luftwaffe* – new pilots were posted to squadrons before they were fit to go into action. In September, 1940, Ginger Lacey, the top-scoring pilot in the Battle of Britain, slept in a room at Biggin Hill that contained four beds. During one four-day perid, three of these were each occupied by two different pilots. In June, 1944, German pilots were being killed at much the same rate. People who have never been associated with military aviation are unaware of the scale of accidents that occur. Collisions in the air or on the ground and forced landings are sometimes caused by weather or mechanical defects, many are the product of inexperience.

The rough airfields from which Galland's fighters now had to operate were overcrowded, which made for frequent accidents. Nearly half the pilots flying to them from Germany were killed or wounded on the way by enemy fighters. Many times, while fighters were on their way to a new field, an enemy attack put it out of commission. The pilots then had to try to find an 'alternate', an American misuse of the word, which should be 'alternative', that has, regrettably, become standard in Service and civil aviation. Because communications were so bad, pilots in need of a diversion could not make contact with the ground controllers who could give them one, so had to make a forced landing. Pilots whose training had been curtailed had done little cross-country flying and were therefore poor navigators, who frequently lost their way. If they did not crash, they arrived in the wrong place. Galland writes, 'There was an incredible number of crashes. The repair squads were so overtaxed that they were unable to get a sufficient number of aircraft back into service or to salvage the crashed ones.'

The result of all this was that the pilots and aircraft of several squadrons were scattered on different airfields and reuniting them was delayed by the destruction of telephone lines and radio equipment.

A major handicap to such operations as could be carried out was that most of the fighters had to be based north-west of Paris, where the ground organization was more compact and less damaged than in the battle zone. They had to approach the beachhead from a flank, which made it easier for defending fighters to patrol and intercept. Galland records, 'Thus most of the dogfights took place far away from the invasion area, not because our fighters preferred it this way, but because the superior Allied forces dictated it so.' The Dunkirk Syndrome again.

Pilot and aircraft losses, dispersion and fragmentation of units meant that few wings now had their original squadrons – some comprised three strange ones. The effect of this has been much underrated; lowering of morale by separation from familiar, tried and tested comrades; loss of efficiency by the imposition of unfamiliar types of operation. About a third of the whole force consisted of fighter-bomber and bomber wings, which came under the 2nd Flying Corps, while the rest of the fighter wings came under the 2nd Fighter Corps. The first of these was a close combat corps, the second an air defence corps; their specialities differed but they had to work closely together.

Galland found that the High Command lacked a sound judgment of the situation and a clear concept of how the few fighters should be used so that they would have some chance of success against odds of twenty to one. Principles of fighting that had been successful in 1940 and on the Russian Front were still being followed, although the circumstances had changed drastically. The High Command plan was for daylight bombing with fighter escort, but the chief of *Luftwaffe* Command in the West, *Generalmajor* Werner Junck, persuaded OKW to cancel this. The new plan was for fighters and fighter-bombers to attack the beachhead continuously. When the Allied fighters thwarted this, a new stratagem was tried. The fighter escort for the fighter-bombers was increased and the approach to the target was made at very high altitude. However, it was seldom possible to assemble the required formation, because the Allies had the German airfields constantly under watch. The fighter-bombers, which had sustained heavy losses, therefore reverted to the role of pure fighters. At the end of June the 2nd Flying Corps was disbanded and its squadrons joined 2nd Fighter Corps, under whose command were also the 4th and 5th Fighter Divisions. By now 1,000 aircraft had been lost on the invasion front, but 998 new ones had replaced them. There was no replacement, though, for the experienced pilots who were dead or wounded.

The German Army had incurred the same kind of loss and damage, breakdown of communications, frustration of plans and sinking of morale, under the guns and bombs of the Allied air forces. Second Tactical Air Force destroyed 551 railway locomotives in June and made any movement of reinforcements from Germany impossible by daylight. The General Commanding the 2nd Panzer Division reported, 'The Allies have total air supremacy. They bomb and shoot at anything that moves, even single vehicles and men. [By the USAAF that all too often included their allies' movements]. Our territory is under constant observation. The feeling of being powerless against the enemy's aircraft has a paralysing effect.'

The unit next above *Gruppe* was *Geschwader*, which comprised three *Gruppen*. Of these larger formations, there were two based in France that had won outstanding distinction, J6 (*Jagdgeschwader*) 2 (Richthofen), named after the famous German fighter ace of the Great War, and JG26 (*Schlageter*), which means Striker in the most vehement sense. JG26, in which Galland had commanded a squadron, a wing, then the *Geschwader* itself, boasted the most distinguished record of all such units. Hauptmann Walter Krupinski was its most successful pilot, with 197 victories. There were fifty others with between 55 and 190. Its *Kommodore* in June, 1944, was *Oberstleutnant* Josef 'Pips' Priller, who was later promoted to full colonel. At the time of the invasion he was twenty-eight years old and had scored 96 victories. On 7 June he shot down a Thunderbolt and a Mustang, on 11 June a Lightning and on 15 June a Liberator. He went on to make one more kill and survived the war.

Descriptions of Priller's ninety-ninth and hundredth victories convey a stark impression of combat and the German fighter pilots' attitude. There is still a desperate bravery against odds that they know are insuperable and there is also the feel of weary men laconically telling the story of monotonously repeated battles in a hopeless conflict.

The first is by *Leutnant* Gerd Wiegand, whose final score was thirty-four. '11.6.44. Take off 1230 – Priller leads – make height behind the battle area; task; to cover various roads – Radio message "Lightnings in the area" – "We're coming" – Four-tenths cloud. See 10 Lightnings at 2000 metres – same height – Climb at full throttle – Get above them – Attack the Lightning formation – Priller shoots a Lightning down – The right-hand section turns – I stay with it – confused twisting and turning – I shoot; Lightning burns – Fly after the others – I am alone, 2000 metres in front of me a Lightning – Further behind – suddenly Lightning changes course – I shoot at once – See hits, then my windscreen black (oil tank hit) – Terrifying bang – Hanging with legs in air – My tail shot off – Parachute – Right thigh hangs swinging from side to side – 6 Lightnings circle parachute – painful bounce on the ground – Field 3 kilometres north of Compiègne – After four hours, first hospital and anaesthetic – Thigh shattered – Goodnight.'

The second is Priller's combat report. 'On 15.6 I took off at 0625 hrs as formation leader of II and III/26 [Second and third *Staffeln* of JG26] from Guyancourt, to patrol in Areas TT8 and UT2.

'At 0650 hrs I saw at 6000-7000 metres altitude, 100 kilometres south of Chartres, flying in threes, a bomber formation of about 70-80 Boeings [B17s] and Liberators, escorted by a very large number of fighters.

'I attacked the first three from the flank at the same height and hit one of the left-hand Boeings. During the ensuing air battle with the very strong fighter escort I made a head-on attack against a formation of about 20 Liberators. I fired at the left-hand Liberator in the leading section from 600–100 metres range and saw hits on the cockpit and both the port-side engines. After breaking off I saw the Liberator on three engines leave the formation with a fierce fire burning in a steep curve and hurtle down. On account of the continuing fight I could not see it hit the ground.'

The third is the combat report by *Unteroffizier* (Sergeant) Heinz Wodarczyk. 'Take off: 0625 hrs. Shooting down: 0710hrs. Landed: 0735 hrs Chartres on account of fuel shortage – 0840 hrs at Guyancourt. On 15.6.1944 I took off as wing man to Lieutenant-Colonel Priller from Guyancourt to patrol in Areas TT8 and UT2. At 0705 hrs we attacked a column of Liberators head-on at the same height. I witnessed how Lieutenant-Colonel Priller fired at the left-hand Liberator in the first section and hit it in the cockpit and the two port engines. The Liberator immediately emitted flames and broke away from the formation in a steep downward curve. I could not see it hit the ground because of the further fighting. The shooting down occurred at 0710 hrs roughly in Area AB–BB.'

The air battle witness's report by *Hauptmann* Walter Matoni, who led 2/JG26, confirmed Priller's claim.

To be a successful fighter pilot despite having had a leg or two amputated was not unique. Colin Hodgkinson of the Fleet Air Arm shared Douglas Bader's misfortune of having lost both limbs. The Italian *Tenente Colonnello* Ernesto 'Iron Leg' Butto had lost one leg when flying for the Fascists in Spain but was still leading fighter formations in the Western Desert in 1940.

Priller recounts the exploits of *Oberleutnant* Viktor Hilgendorf, JG26's oldest pilot at 29, who shot down two hostiles after his amputation. He had joined the unit in 1941 and flew as Galland's No 2, wing man, *Rottenflieger* or *Katschmarek*. He was shot down the next year on his forty-first operational sortie, with one victory to his name, and wounded in both legs. The right one had to be taken off above the knee. A two-centimetre length of bone had been shot out of the left shin, which had to be joined. After eighteen months in hospital he rejoined the *Geschwader*.

To begin with he was made Technical Officer of the *Gruppe* with the hidden intention of preventing him flying. In any event he was forbidden to take part in operations.

He was so persistent in his requests to have this embargo rescinded that, on 10 May, 1944, he found himself leading No 9 *Staffel*. That is an indication of the gravity of the German Air Force's situation and the dearth of experienced pilots, let alone leaders. Between then and 7 June he flew on ten operations. A week later he had to bale out when his aircraft was set on fire. His artificial leg came off and he tucked it under his arm as he drifted down to earth. In landing he fractured a hip. A week later he flew again and on 7 July shot down his second enemy aircraft, a Mustang. He was killed in action next day. Priller says he was an open, tough and energetic man, remembered for his cheerful nature and sense of humour.

The invasion blasted into the lives of the German fighter pilots in France like the peremptory outburst of a tart withdrawing her favours from a rich libertine who has suddenly become bankrupt. In the sombre summer weeks of 1940, after the *Blitzkrieg* had stormed its way across the country, flattened the French Army and driven the British Expeditionary Force into the sea, there had been a period of general resentment and loathing. Soon this was subtly infused by the kind of reconciliation with some sections of a population that follows every conquest. As the years passed, the number of French people who associated willingly with Germans grew, but remained a very small proportion of the population.

Young women who depended for their living on public favour – entertainers, in the broadest sense, on the stage, in night clubs or flat on their backs – had to be smiling, friendly and complaisant or go hungry. For others, the contrast between the smart, beefy young conquerors full of confidence and the shabby, underfed vanquished was magnetic. The stale apophthegm that power is the great aphrodisiac was exemplified to some degree in every downtrodden occupied country. When the young aircrew, well fed and exuding feral healthiness, looking like romantic leads in a musical film with their widely pegged riding breeches and jackboots, went out for a night on the town, they found willing partners to dance with and more. They lived comfortably at permanent French Air Force stations or in requisitioned châteaux, guzzled wine that was too good for their palates and found cognac and armagnac superior to German brandy.

Now they were living in tents on airfields, rented rooms in the homes of unfriendly people who prayed for their defeat, or requisitioned houses near their temporary bases. They were reeling from the shock of heavy losses during the past six months and the battering that had been inflicted on them since 6 June. There was scant energy left for chasing girls. Carousing in an extempore mess was damped by despair for the future and the knowledge that an aching head and reactions dulled by rising before dawn could be fatal.

Recognition of approaching doom did not sap the German airmen's fighting spirit, but confidence in ultimate victory changed to a desperate determination to stave off defeat as long as one serviceable aircraft and one round of ammunition remained. This mood had germinated early in what turned out to be the invasion year. For most it was patriotism and personal honour. For others it was fanaticism. *Hauptmann* Heinz Knoke, who was married with two small children and commanded a *Staffel* in KG11, was a prime example of the kind of young man who, until the end, was prepared to give his life for Hitler.

His diary entry on 4 January, 1944, begins 'For nearly a week the Fortresses have left us in peace. Today the concentrations are again reported'. At 1002 hrs the *Geschwader* took off for the first mission of the new year. They attacked a strong formation of B17s escorted by P47s that were already under fire from flak. A shell hit his aircraft and tore off half the engine. A P47's bullets hit his wing, which caught fire. He jettisoned the canopy, but before he could bale out he was sucked out of the cockpit. His parachute was snagged, his right leg was out of the aeroplane and the left inside it. After falling several thousand feet he released himself and as he fell free he felt heavy blows on his back and head. He had sustained a fractured skull and lumbar vertebrae, severe bruising of shoulders and pelvis, a wound under the hip, severe concussion and temporary paralysis of the right side. When he next flew, to intercept a bomber formation escorted by Spitfires on 30 January, he hobbled to his Me109 on crutches. The Messerchmitts lost nine pilots and shot down one Spitfire.

He wrote in his diary: 'The Americans and Britsh conduct their large-scale operations in a way that leaves us no respite. They have rained hundreds of thousands of tons of high explosive and phosphorous incendiary bombs upon our cities and industrial centres. Night after night the wail of the sirens heralds more raids. How much longer can it all continue?'

On 8 March the JG's *Kommodore* requested that it should be temporarily withdrawn from operations because his pilots could not continue. He was refused. Knoke's diary entry is, 'We are to continue flying to the last aircraft and the last pilot. It has become very silent in the crew room. Jonny Fest and I sit there alone in our armchairs until far into the night. We do not speak. The pile of cigarette butts in the ashtray grows steadily. Jonny keeps staring in a *distrait* way at the pictures on the wall. To me it seems as if we might expect to see the faces move and hear the familiar voices of our late comrades break the silence in the room.'

Then follows a morbid, maudlin litany typical of his race.

'Wolny – We were returning from his funeral in the Chief's car when a girl suddenly dashed into the road carrying a wreath. It was his fiancée. She had been ashamed to stand beside us at the grave because she was afraid that she still could not control the grief that overwhelmed her when told of his death three days before.

'Steiger – looked exactly like his twin brother. I met him last year and at first thought it was Gerd.

'Kolbe – they found his body in the wreckage, minus both hands. Then his wife asked for the wedding ring. How could we possibly tell her the truth?

'Krame – why, oh why, did that boy have to lose his head that time his aircraft went down in the sea?

'Gerhard – his mother writes to me often and I have to tell her all about her brave son.

'Killian – his perpetual affairs with women caused me plenty of trouble.

'Führmann – on the spot where his Messerschmitt carried him down when it plunged into the moor we erected a tall oak cross. At its base we nailed two five-franc pieces.' He does not explain the significance of this esoteric or pagan tribute.

'Nowotny – his father wrote to me that two of his brothers had also been killed in action.

'Raddatz – his darling Myra-Lydia shed tears at the time, but did not take long to find consolation elsewhere. Still, she was not the only one to find his charms irresistible.

'Reinhardt – my good old buddy once showed me a photograph of his six brothers and himself, all together, all in uniform and all wearing the Iron Cross First Class.'

And so it rambles on until, 'Now only Jonny and I remain.'

A week later, 15 March, '0955 hrs take off to intercept. Six aircraft: four return. This is the end.'

A message comes that the unit is to be rested from operations. 'I produce a bottle.'

'"Let us make it a proper celebration tonight," Jonny suggests.

'It seems like a good idea. We roll and zigzag through the streets, singing and shouting. Luckily it is dark. Jonny knows a young widow living in town. We go up to her place. She invites her girl friend over. Then we drink and dance until our feet no longer support us. Nothing matters now, except to get away from it all and to be able just for a little while to forget. I spend the night in a strange bed.'

On 29 April he is in action again. 'The escort are Lightnings, Thunderbolts and Mustangs. The heavy bombers are strung out as far as the eye can reach.' Soon, 'We are in a madly whirling dogfight. Our job is done; it is a case of every man for himself. I remain on the tail of a Lightning. It flies like the devil himself, turning, diving and climbing almost like a rocket. I am never able to fire more than a few potshots. Then a flight of Mustangs dives past. Tracers whistle past my head. I pull back the stick with both hands and the aircraft climbs steeply out of the way. My wing man, Sergeant Drühe, remains close to my tail.

'Once again I have a chance to fire at a Lightning. My salvoes register at last. Smoke billows out of the right engine. I have to break away. I have eight Thunderbolts on my tail. The enemy tracers again come past my head. I use my emergency boost and try to get away. The bastards are still on my tail, firing, I do not know how they miss, but they do. I get a Yank in my sights, open fire with all guns, the crate goes up in a steep climb. Then all his comrades are back on my tail. One moment I am thrust down into the seat in a tight turn, the next I am upside down, hanging in my safety harness with my head practically touching the canopy roof and the guts coming into my mouth.'

He gets away, but, 'There are eight Thunderbolts on my tail. Their salvoes slam into my aircraft. My right wing bursts into flame. A Thunderbolt looms ahead, I open fire. Its tail is soon in flames.' His aircraft is on fire and he is about to bale out when the burning Thunderbolt puts more bullets into it. 'I shall be chewed to mincemeat by the airscrew if I try to bale out now. I huddle down and crouch low in my seat. A large hole gapes beside my right leg, the instrument panel flies into splinters. I feel the heat of the flames.'

The Thunderbolt crosses in front of him. He fires again and its pilot bales out.

'It is too late for me to bale out now. I cross some large fields. Down goes the nose and the aircraft settles. The flames come up, reaching for my face. Earth flies into the air. There is a dull, heavy thud. Something crashes with stunning force into my head.'

He climbed out, held his aching head in both hands and sank to his knees. 'The world spins crazily in front of my eyes. I am overcome by recurrent nausea, until only the taste of green bile remains. The other seven Thunderbolts keep diving at me, firing. It seems a long way to the edge of the field, I roll into the ditch and pass out.'

The accusation of the Thunderbolt pilots' ineptitude is dubious. It seems unlikely that eight aircraft, each armed with eight .05 inch machine guns, could have missed him.

He regained consciousness to find a tall American standing over him. They sat side by side on the edge of the ditch, offered each other cigarettes, which both refused, and talked. The tone of the diary entry changes from bitter disappointment at the steady erosion of the *Luftwaffe* and queasy sentimentality about dead comrades to a bluff matiness. This is at least a trifle equivocal, although it is true that RAF and German fighter pilots who were shot down and taken prisoner were treated with empathy and chivalry by their adversaries.

The American asked, 'Was that you flying the Messerschmitt?'

'Yes.'

'You wounded?'

'Feels like it.'

'The back of your head is bleeding.'

Knoke could feel blood trickling down his neck.

The American continued, 'Did you really shoot me down?'

'Yes.'

'But I don't see how you could. Your airplane was a mass of flames.'

'Don't I know it!'

'It sure seemed like a bit of luck when I spotted you above the clouds and we all went after you.'

'What was your idea in getting in front of me when my engine died?'

'Too much forward speed. Besides, it never occurred to me that you would still be firing.'

'That is where you made your mistake.'

The American laughed. 'Guess I'm not the first you bagged, am I?'

'No, you are my twenty-sixth.'

The American declared that he had a score of seventeen. He was due to go home soon, but that would have to be postponed until he was released from prison camp. He told Knoke that he was married. So Knoke showed him a photograph of his own wife and children.

'We have a friendly chat for about half an hour. He seems like a decent fellow.' He expatiates on this unctuous admission: 'There is no suggestion of hatred between us, nor any reason for it. We have too much in common. We are both pilots and we have both narrowly escaped death.'

A lorry carrying the six survivors from a B17 fetches them and drives them to the airfield, picking up more Americans on the way. 'I try to cheer up the party with a few jokes.' At their destination, 'I say farewell to my fellow sufferers and we all shake hands.'

That night Knoke was admitted to hospital, unconscious and with 'a raging fever'.

On 11 August he returned to flying duties, posted to command IIIJG1. He resumed the ineluctable struggle at once, the everlasting allure of aggression. Why else does anyone choose a combatant Service as a career?

In the morning a reconnaissance fighter flew over. Knoke's comment was, 'The bastard is going to set his bomber comrades on to us! Sure enough, eight fighter bombers appear an hour later and strafe the dispersal area, destroying one of our aircraft. Before the dust has time to settle, I am out of my camouflaged shelter and take off in pursuit. Instead of catching them I shoot down a Lightning which is flying alone, apparently on reconnaissance.

'In the evening the runway suddenly erupts in geysers of earth, just when we return from operations against the advancing American tanks and are about to land. Then I notice, shimmering in the hot sky overhead, a pack of some twelve Marauders [B26]. We attack them, although fuel is running dangerously low. My men shoot three down and a fourth is credited to me. We are obliged to land at Bretigny, because of the number of deep craters on our runway. During the night the squadron moves to another airfield.'

The telephone wakes him at 0300, as it does every morning,

and he is given his operational orders. He flies four times that day and brings down three Thunderbolts.

'But what is the use? Five of our aircraft do not return. That is bad for us. The loss of five aircraft, or five pilots, means as much as a loss of fifty to the enemy.'

12

MORE AIRFIELDS BECOME OPERATIONAL

By D-plus-10 twelve airfields were ready for use in the British sector and the same number in the American, and still the work went on. Throughout, artillery fire and, when cloud base was low enough to prevent Allied fighters patrolling at altitude, attacks by FW190 and Me109 fighter bombers roaring in at nought feet were frequent. The RAF Regiment's 40mm Bofors guns that defended the British airfields notched up a good tally of successes whatever the weather. By the end of June all 83 Group wings were based in Normandy. The defenders were still confined close to the beachhead, a proximity that deprived the attacking side of sleep. After a hard day's work in the air or on the ground, air and maintenance crews found their nights constantly disturbed by both enemy and friendly gunfire and shell bursts and the explosion of bombs dropped by the RAF.

The ground crews of 137 (Typhoon) Squadron at Manston in Kent were loading the DC3 Dakotas that were to fly them across the Channel. Technical officers and NCOs supervised, exhorting them to handle the cargo carefully. When the squadron completed its move to France it would not be possible to replace damaged spare parts, workshop equipment and other essential materiel as quickly as could be done while at home.

The task completed, everyone went aboard to make the journey sitting on the baggage. They flew without parachutes or life jackets, which might have proved an unwise display of confidence in Allied air superiority. But no enemy fighters slipped past the interception fighters that patrolled over the Normandy coast. When they landed at B6 airfield, however, where the pilots and their Typhoons had preceded them, shells were zipping overhead. Officers and NCOs abandoned their solicitude for gentle treatment of technical stores.

D. V.(Des) Davies, a flight mechanic (engines), remembers that caution and chiding were replaced by three words, 'Throw it out'. The troops did so with a will – not so that they might find shelter in a slit trench, but to enable the Dakotas to take off as soon as possible, before shells started to drop on them.

The squadron flew daily from dawn to dusk, continuing the task of rocketing enemy armour that it had begun while based in England. Now, however, there was an inconvenience that had been absent in Kent: 'Our own artillery shelling over our heads in one direction and the Germans shelling in the opposite direction. We lost a number of Typhoons and pilots as they were landing, because of it. We also had to be alert for snipers in the orchards.'

In common with everyone else on all the landing strips, theirs was a life of work, eat and sleep, 'The only instance of time off was when four or five of us at a time were allowed (once) to have a couple of hours in Bayeux.'

It was the start of six months during which Aircraftman Davies and his comrades in ground trades were daily exposed to enemy attack, even when they had advanced far beyond the Normandy beachhead. Fighter squadrons, whether bombing and rocketing enemy positions on the ground or intercepting enemy aircraft overhead, pressed ahead fast on the heels of the Army as it won terrain from the retreating defenders. Their airfields were always close to the front.

What befell Des Davies half a year after he jumped out of a Dakota on to French soil and began hastily unloading freight while shells were bursting a couple of hundred yards away could have happened at any time. The squadron had fought its way to Holland. At about 0930 on 1 January, 1945, some fifty Me109s and FW190s strafed the airfield. Most of 137's Typhoons had just taken off and another squadron was at the down-wind end of the runway, ready to follow.

Aircraftman Davies takes up the story: 'In the next half hour many RAF men were klled and wounded. Pilots trying to get out of aircraft near the runway (now being unable to take off) were machine-gunned. One pilot taxiing his aircraft was killed in the cockpit. The flight sergeant in charge of ground staff on my squadron was killed, his stomach ripped open by cannon shells. I ended up diving under a three-ton truck and was continually attacked there and was hit in the leg, smashing the bone. When it all eventually ended I was lying in a pool of my own blood. The airfield was burning everywhere, with ammunition and rockets exploding. When dragged from under the truck, its steel side nine inches or so above my head was full of cannon shell holes. I was taken to the casualty clearing station, given a shot of morphia, my field dressing was left covering the wound.'

He was then taken to an improvised hospital and operated on. That night an ambulance train carried him away from the forward area and he was soon in another hospital and then yet another. He was told that penicillin, which was just coming into use, had saved his leg from amputation. 'I have since often wished it had been. I am still in a lot of pain with it to this day. Six months and five operations later, I returned to my squadron, only to find I could no longer do my job.'

It was an unhappy start to a new year, but his luck could have run out on any of the one hundred and eighty or so days and nights since he entered the shooting war.

He was still only nineteen years old.

On 13 June two French squadrons, 340 and 341, had landed at B5 to refuel and re-arm. One of the pilots describes their feelings. 'Some kissed the ground, others, made awkward by their emotions, found everything they saw more beautiful than in England; the grass more lush, the soil richer. This steeple, what a marvel of Christian simplicity! These peasants with their sly faces, what fine people! Everyone overflowed with infinite tenderness. But the war was present and there was no question of lingering in the farmyards drinking cider. In the afternoon they had to take off again from that small airfield at St Croix.'

Six days later 329 Squadron followed them on a short visit home. The first patrol, in the morning, passed without incident. The afternoon one was equally uneventful. One of the pilots remembers, 'We were ordered to land in France instead of returning to England, an order that did not need to be repeated, even for the section that found itself already half-way across the Channel on its way back and made an about turn. There were some complications concerning the landing field, for the area abounded with them and each had to make his own choice.

'Lieutenant-Colonel Fleurquin, Captain Marchelidon, Lieutenants Avon and Muzard, Sergeant-Major Lombaert put down at St Croix, while Lieutenant Tanguy, followed by Saigne and Alligier landed near Bayeux.

'At last we were in France, breathing French dust (and God knows there was plenty of it). But the most moving thing was the welcome by the French people who were there. Their spontaneous displays of joy made a profound impression on us. They were doubly happy to be at last delivered from German oppression and to see French airmen among their liberators. More than one of them started to snivel "the product of their lachrymal glands". We were assailed by handshakes, congratulations and everyone tried to pin a souvenir to our battledress; a cross of Lorraine, small French flags, mascots of all sorts. Unhappily, the pilots were unable to linger, for the weather was worsening on the other side of the Channel. On the way back an error in navigation led the formation towards the anti-aircraft defence zone on the south coast of England; a mistake that was corrected in time.'

On 19 June 345 Squadron, still using its English base, earned praise from its Wing Leader, Wing Commander D. E. Kingaby, DSO, DFM and two bars, and the Station Commander, Group Captain Crisham, for being the only one of the Shoreham squadrons to have arrived with perfect punctuality every time they relieved another on patrol.

Don Kingaby had started the war as a Volunteer Reserve sergeant pilot. By June, 1944, he had shot down twenty-three enemy aircraft, scored eight probables and damaged sixteen. He went on to become a group captain.

A reminiscence of Crisham might enliven the sorry story of pilots lost in the Channel earlier that month. He was a keen racing man who, when commanding Kirton Lindsey, a fighter sector in Lincolnshire, used to fly a Tiger Moth to race meetings and land on the area surrounded by the course. One winter evening after dark, when the group captain had taken off on his homeward flight, the weather deteriorated and low cloud covered the county and neighbouring Yorkshire. In RAF lingo it was 'clampers' – clamped in. The Tannoy loudspeakers all over the camp announced that he had crashed somewhere nearby and called for volunteers to search for him. He was soon found, unharmed except for losing a tooth that was embedded in the instrument panel when the impact threw him face-first against it. 'Now,' said an airman who had spent an hour tramping through the murk looking for the wreckage, 'Groupie can say "at last I've really got my teeth into this flying business".'

The first time the RAF and USAAF shared an operation after the invasion was in support of the US Seventh Corps when Cherbourg was taken. At noon on 22 June four Typhoon squadrons rocketed the flak batteries on which six Mustang squadrons dropped 1000lb bombs before strafing with cannon. At 1330 hrs 557 USAAF Lightnings and Thunderbolts went in with 500-pounders.

On 25 June 746 fighter-bombers and fighters, 416 of which were based on Normandy airfields, attacked enemy positions west of Caen, in preparation.

On 27 June there was ten-tenths low cloud and the rain was pelting down. In theory the weather was non-operational, but the Second British Army was heavily attacking Odon, and in response to urgent requests from the Eighth Corps, 115 Typhoons rocketed bridges, tanks hiding behind hedges, anti-tank guns and mortars. They also attacked hangars on Carpiquet airfield, where tanks were sheltering. During the night 223 Lancasters and Halifaxes bombed the railway stations at Vitry-le-François, Bar-le-Duc and Vierzon, through which the Second SS Panzer Korps was due to pass.

On 28 June 200 German fighters appeared in the Normandy sky, supporting a German counter-attack. The Canadian Wing brought down twelve of them.

On 29 June 2nd TAF flew 637 ground-attack sorties, the greatest number to date from French bases. From English bases a further 600 sorties were flown over Normandy.

On the last day of the month the *Luftwaffe* astonishingly managed to fly 600 sorties with only some 200 aircraft serviceable. Second TAF flew 1,040.

13

A MOBILE RADAR BEACON
COMES ASHORE TO A HOT SPOT

Among the mobile RAF units that were essential to operations were the Air Ministry Experimental Stations (AMES), a vague designation that concealed various forms of radar. Some gave early warning of the distance and height of enemy aircraft, some were used to control friendly fighters that were intercepting them. Others, the eight Radar and Mobile Signals Units (RAMSU), operated a device called an Eureka-H beacon. This was a navigation aid used mainly by night photographic reconnaissance aircraft, which carried another radar instrument, Rebecca-H.

The Rebecca-Eureka equipment had been designed to enable troop transport aircraft to home on to a portable Eureka beacon already put in place by pathfinder paratroops, so that the gliders could land accurately on the dropping zone (See Chapter 4).

Both airborne and ground-based equipments used identical transmitters and receivers, which operated at five spot frequencies from 214 MHz to 234 MHz at 5 MHz intervals. The aircraft transmitted four-microsecond, 200 Watt pulses, 300 times a second at one of the spot frequencies. A few microseconds after receiving an aircraft's pulse, the beacon would transmit a similar pulse on one of the other spot frequencies. Although the replies were automatic, earphones were used on the ground-based set to indicate to the operator that the beacon was being interrogated. In order to differentiate between the beacons, each would automatically interrupt its replies once per minute. During this brief interlude the equipment would code its reply pulses with a Morse character – RAMSU 5320 transmitted 'A'.

The aircraft equipment comprised a transmitter-receiver unit, a timing unit and a display unit. The display unit used a cathode ray tube which showed range on its vertical axis. The navigator had a choice of four ranges in nautical miles (nm), two of which, fourteen-mile and seventy-mile, were used consistently in a reconnaissance role. The display unit also had a mechanical pointer on each side of the centre sweeping line that could be adjusted vertically. The timing unit initiated the trigger pulse to the transmitter unit, and undelayed and delayed pulses to the display unit. It had two knobs, labelled in steps of ten from zero to 110 nautical miles, which provided corresponding delayed trigger pulses to the display unit.

The aircraft navigator was briefed on the ranges of the target from two beacons. If, for example, it was 66.8 nm from beacon A and 44.8 nm from beacon B, he would set the left-hand range knob of the timing unit to 60 and the right-hand one to 40. The left-hand pointer on the display unit would be set to 6.8 and the right-hand one to 4.8 on the 14-mile range.

Initially using the 70 nm range on the display unit, he would direct the pilot to a point approximately 66.8 nm from beacon A, identified on the display by its Morse character. At an appropriate time the navigator would switch to the 14-mile range and the signal from beacon A would then appear only on the left-hand side of the trace. Using the left-hand pointer as a reference, he would direct the pilot to fly a course such that beacon A's signal always appeared under the pointer i.e. the aircraft was always at constant range from beacon A. As the pilot flew this course, the signal from beacon B would finally appear on the display unit as a deflection of the cathode ray tube trace to the right. It could appear at either the top or bottom of the trace, dependent on the tactics decided upon at briefing. The signal from beacon B would drift along the trace until it was under the right-hand pointer. The navigator would then press a button and a series of photographs of the area below the aircraft would be taken, using photo flares.

The aircraft's base also had an Eureka beacon on it or close by, and the aircraft was fitted with homing antennae for easy navigation on its return.

The beacons operated with 34 Wing, the Headquarters Wing of 2nd TAF. By D-Day the Wing consisted of 140 Squadron, flying Mosquito XVIs, 69 flying Wellington X111s, both on photo recce and based at Northolt, and 1401 Meteorological Flight, operating high altitude Spitfire 1Xs, stationed at Manston.

Geoffrey Merriman was corporal in charge of RAMSU 5320 – a considerable disjunction from his career before and after the war in marine and aircraft insurance. Canadian radar mechanic, Corporal F. R. Hunt (later Dr and a distinguished scientist working for the Canadian Government), was his No 2.

On 25 June the unit sailed from Tilbury aboard the *Fort Biloxi*, a Liberty Ship, and dropped anchor off Arromanches at dusk the next day. Unloading began the following day and on 28 June the vehicles carrying the beacons were transferred to an LCT and went ashore. On 2 July the unit moved to its first operational site, north of Caen and a mile from Hermanville, on the north side of a hill. The domestic site was about a mile south, on the other side.

Dr Hunt writes, 'The living site was in the midst of about two hundred guns ranging from 75mm to anti-aircraft. They all appeared to fire simultaneously every hour. Periodically sixteen-inch shells from a warship lying offshore passed overhead sounding much like a freight train in the sky.'

The unit subsisted on the usual compo rations – tinned food sufficient for fourteen men for one day. 'They appeared to consist only of fish, corned beef, steak and kidney stew, marmalade and puddings.' On the first night it was raining, so they slept in abandoned foxholes.

Next day orders came for the positioning of the technical truck on a site that was 'in full view of the Germans', who were about four kilometres away., At sunset the following day they had an indication of their neighbours' unfriendliness.

To quote Dr Hunt's record of those days: 'Corporal Merriman

and I climbed into the technical vehicle prior to moving up to the tech site. I started the engine and was warming it up. "Bam" and something hopped along the ground like a running rabbit. We realized very quickly that it was not a rabbit and hopped out of the truck and made for our nearby dugout. The shelling continued for fifteen minutes at about fifteen-second intervals. After the shelling ceased we moved up to the tech site. The technical vehicle had only a small dent in one side. The remainder of our vehicles had not been touched, but an ammunition truck was burning across the road.'

The next morning another site was found. They were about to move the beacon when the shelling started again. There were no foxholes nearby, so they lay under the truck, with its petrol tanks directly above them. There was a herd of cows in the field and two were killed a few yards from the corporals' temporary – and highly flammable – shelter.

In the Second Century A.D., Marcus Aurelius reflected in his Meditations: 'Nothing can happen unto thee, which is not incidental unto thee, as thou art a man. As nothing can happen either to an ox, a vine, or to a stone, which is not incidental unto them; unto every one in his own kind': including wartime airmen in trades not usually associated in the public mind with battle and sudden death – and, on the evidence, French cattle at pasture.

14

JULY – A CRITICAL TIME

On 25 July Lady Grant Lawson, 345 Squadron's 'God-mother', visited them and, the squadron records show, distributed cartons of 'excellent American cigarettes, a much appreciated gift. Her visit brought *Berry* good luck. Next morning, after a patrol over Normandy, the squadron was ordered to land at B2 on account of the bad weather in England. The pilots, crazy with delight, looked forward to dispersing among the farms and villages. Captain Guizard had trouble in preventing them, as they had to stay in their cockpits at stand-by. 'Three of them, all the same, managed a visit to the village and reappeared with camembert, real Isigny butter and bottles of cider, which were consumed on the spot.'

In August they joined Nos 91 – a British – Squadron and 322 (Dutch) as 141 Wing. They were re-equipped with Spitfire 1Xs, which had two 20mm cannon and four, 303 machine guns, 'an armament more comfortable [than the Spit VA's eight m/gs] for confronting Me109s and FW190s'. It was not until October that they were transferred to a French base, Courtrai, to relieve 340 Squadron.

Ecstatically though the locals welcomed the sight of their compatriots, they were less than enthusiastic about the arrival of Britons and Americans. Their scarcely perceptible gratitude has been described as 'a trifle hesitant'. The reason was the loss of stock occasioned by bombs and shells and of crops when the bulldozer got to work clearing the ground. Their equivocal attitude evokes the cynical supposition that they were not sure the Allies were there to stay. Remembering the thundering German might in 1940, they were ready for the invaders to be thrown back into the sea at any moment. When it became obvious that this was not going to happen, smiles began to replace the sullen bucolic resignation.

The RAF set up a cinema screen in a barn near B5 and films were shown, to which the peasantry were invited. Ignorance of English did not inhibit their attendance. The Medical and Dental Branches opened a village clinic and civilians flocked there; some to have wounds and broken bones, incurred from bomb and shell fragments and the blast, attended to, others for the normal ailments to which GPs are accustomed. Even midwifery services were rendered.

Recreational facilities for officers and men were few. On some airfields two-stroke motorcycles that had been dropped with other paratroop equipment were used for short runs around the countryside. Pilots could find a little time between sorties, sometimes on account of non-flying weather, but the maintenance crews had to work even when aircraft were grounded.

Living conditions were as rough as they still were in Burma and had been in the desert, Sicily and the early days in Italy, but at least the climate was temperate. Water was scarce, so the facility known in the RAF as 'ablutions' was primitive. Rations remained monotonous and minimal.

June had ended with Caen, the major obstacle in the Allies' path, still uncaptured. Until it fell, General Sir Miles Dempsey, commanding the 2nd Army, could not use the roads that led through it to position his force in strength enough to contain the German armour confronting him. The German Generals knew that the city was untenable, but Hitler insisted that they must stand firm. Dempsey had no alternative to a frontal attack. Its first phase, capture of the village of Carpiquet on 4 July, succeeded; but the airfield there was defended by the SS, who did not succumb.

On 7 July 2nd TAF flew 766 sorties in support of the ground forces investing the city. To minimize casualties and to accomplish the task as quickly as possible, Dempsey asked the RAF to bomb Caen. That night 467 Lancasters and Halifaxes dropped 2,560 tons of high explosive on its northern suburbs. Unavoidably, there was great destruction in residential districts and loss of civilian lives. Despite the damage, the enemy was able to hold on to the outskirts, now inaccesible to the Allied tanks until bulldozers could clear the streets of Caen, which were littered with rubble.

The next day 2nd TAF flew 490 sorties. This made a daily average of 390 during the thirty days since the first Normandy airfield came into use.

On 9 July Caen was taken, but fighting went on in its northern fringe.

By mid-July the front extended from eight miles east of Caen to Lessay, in the Cotentin Peninsula. Bombs fell at random, many of them on friendly positions. A fighter bomber pilot who misidentified an RAF airfield and attacked it hit the ammunition dump. A B24 bomabadier accidentally toggled his bomb release over another American airfield, destroyed two medium bombers and their crews and damaged others. The bomb aimer leading another formation dropped his load prematurely, whereupon the fifteen aeroplanes behind him followed suit: 25 men of the 30th US Infantry Division were killed and 131 wounded. The ground assault was postponed until the next day.

The ground forces' positions were marked with yellow panels, an inheritance from the Great War, but they might just as well have been displaying swastikas.

Spectators of these miscarriages in the sky were also entertained one afternoon by an eccentric aerial performance given by a B24 that was on its way back to England with flak damage, including the loss of an engine, which prompted its captain to order the crew to bale out. He trimmed the aircraft nose down and locked the controls so that the autopilot would fly the Liberator on a southerly course, expecting it to crash into the Channel. 'George' was not in obedient mood. The aircraft went first into a steep dive, then soared steeply, banked at the top of its climb and dived again. It repeated this sequence for a quarter of an hour, losing altitude. Two USAAF P47s took potshots at it to try to shoot it down while it was over open country and not a village or airfield; it was unnervingly close to B5. Their aim was no better than their bomber buddies', but the B24's final dive caused no loss of life when it came down on arable land and blew up.

Frequent mistakes continued throughout the campaign. This seems inevitable when thousands of men who have received a wartime training that cannot be as thorough as that of peacetime regulars and reservists are jostling each other in a crowded sky. Add to this the distraction of anti-aircraft shells, 20mm to 88mm in calibre, exploding all around and of strikes on one's aircraft, and most transgressions become less blameable.

On 18 July the British and Canadians opened a major assault from east of the Orne southwards towards the high ground beyond Caen. The push was preceded by 2,200 RAF and USAAF heavy bombers, among them 1,000 Lancasters and Halifaxes that delivered 7,000 tons of bombs on the enemy. The defenders were much confused and demoralized, but poor visibility due to the dust raised by the bombing, shelling and motor vehicles caused confusion among the divisions that were following up the bombardment. On the next day the last Germans in Caen retreated from the eastern suburb of Vaucelles.

On 25 July a massive operation codenamed Cobra was launched. Why this repellent name was chosen is a matter for pychiatrists to explain. The high hopes placed on it were blighted by one of the greatest calamities of the war, and it is now associated with obloquy and ridicule, not triumph. It stands as a monumental error in the annals of 'creep back' or 'short bombing' – dropping bombs short of the target or bomb line. The latter is a line, given in map co-ordinates, within which one's own air force is forbidden to bomb because the ground on that side of it is held by friendly forces. On this morning the front ran from Lessay, on the west of the Cotentin Peninsula, to eight miles east of Caen. The bomb line was the south side of the St Lô–Perrières road. This was as easy a boundary to spot as any airman could wish for; no co-ordinates to bother about, just a straightforward length of highway.

The plan called for the carpet bombing of an area three and a half miles long and one and a half wide, which should kill or stun, alarm and disorient, deafen and blind – with dust – the defending Germans. Immediately after, the Allies would advance rapidly. This was preceded by 2nd TAF fighter-bomber attacks and an artillery barrage that opened fire at 0940.

It was not to be. The USAAF despatched 1,600 bombers to do the job, but rain and low cloud forced their recall. Some aircraft captains heard the message and abandoned the mission. Some either did not receive it or had already bombed. Casualties were twenty-five ground troops killed and 131 wounded. There was considerable retaliatory fire but no record is available of its effect.

On 25 July a second attempt was made. The weather was fine, so at 1000 hrs 1,800 B17s and B24s made the renewed attack. General Omar Bradley, Commanding US forces in Normandy, had made the obvious request that they would make their bombing run from east to west, parallel with the bomb line. It should not have been necessary. Anyone with an IQ above minus would be expected to work out the obvious line of attack without prompting.

Unfortunately there appeared to be a certain lack of intelligence in operation. The bombers came in from north to south, thus maximizing the chances of hitting their own troops. The German 88mm flak put up a hellish barrage and the sky was soon adorned by parachutes and burning aircraft. The ground forces' positions were marked by yellow panels, but in keeping with their usual practice, the bomber crews were flying too high to see them. The first wave of bombers did drop red smoke flares as aiming marks, but their smoke mingled with that from the bomb bursts. Thereupon, the succeeding waves of aeroplanes bombed this drifting smoke – which a five-knot wind was carrying over the bomb line to the Allied side. In the ensuing shambles, although enormous casualties and the destruction of tanks, guns and vehicles were inflicted on the enemy, 101 Americans were killed. One of these was their own Lieutenant-General McNair Wilson, who had imprudently come from Washington specifically to see the show. A further 463 American solders were wounded.

Always there were Allied fighters over the beachhead to protect the ships that were unloading reinforcements, supplies and transport day after day from dawn to dusk. By the end of July the British had put 663,295 men ashore, 156,025 vehicles and 744,540 tons of materiel. The Americans had landed 903,061 men, 176,620 vehicles and 858,436 tons of stores.

Every attack by armour and infantry was preceded by ground strafing and bombing. First the Typhoons, Spitfires and Thunderbolts went in to scour the enemy positions with rockets or bombs and cannon, then the Mitchells and Bostons dropped high explosive and anti-personnel bombs.

Generalleutnant Fritz Bayerlein, commanding the *Panzer Lehr* Division, described the effect of this before the great assault that opened on 25 July; 'The aeroplanes kept coming over as though on a conveyor belt and the bomb carpets unrolled in great rectangles. My flak had hardly opened its mouth when the batteries received direct hits that knocked out half the guns and silenced the rest. After an hour I had no communication with anybody, even by radio. By noon nothing was visible but dust and smoke. My front line looked like the face of the moon and at least seventy per cent of my troops were out of action, dead, wounded, crazed or numbed. All my forward tanks were knocked out and the roads practically impassable.'

15

AUGUST – A MONTH OF
FATAL ERRORS

B etween 7 and 16 August the fighting was concentrated on the Falaise Pocket, a salient thirty-five miles deep and about the same at its widest part that protruded into the area held by the Allies between Caen and Falaise twenty miles due south. The 1st Canadian and 2nd British Armies had driven the enemy back in the north of the pocket, while the US 1st and 3rd Armies had done the same in the south. If the Allies could close the eighteen-mile gap at the eastern end of the pocket they would trap the German 7th Army and nine of the eleven Panzer Divisions that were in France. The German Generals knew that the only sensilble decision was to retreat and again told Hitler so. He forbade it. Eventually they did make a fighting with-drawal but left 100,000 troops in the pocket. Those who had pulled out suffered heavily and most of their tanks, vehicles and guns were destroyed before they reached the Seine.

On 7 August five German Panzer columns comprising 400 tanks opened an advance against the Americans – General Patton's 3rd Army – towards Avranches and the coast. Frustrating them provided an excellent example of inter-allied co-operation. The USAAF had no aircraft that were so effective against tanks as rocket-firing Typhoons. These were engaged throughout the day in support of Patton's troops; a service that was recognized by the award of many US decorations to 2nd TAF pilots.

On 245 Squadron's first mission that day Flight Lieutenant R. Lee was wounded and his engine shot up so badly that he had to make a forced landing on ground between the Allied and enemy lines. Thus began one of the most harrowing experiences ever undergone by a fighter pilot. The Typhoon turned upside down and Lee broke his leg. With extreme difficulty and pain from his injuries, he contrived to unbuckle his safety harness and turn himself the right way up – with the cockpit floor touching his head. The cockpit rim was embedded in the ground and he was unable to crawl out. He began hammering on the side of the fuselage to attract help. He did manage to draw attention to himself; German infantry sportingly opened fire on the wreckage and wounded him further. He kept himself alive on his emergency rations and determination – until, *a week later*, he heard voices speaking English. He gathered his remaining strength to knock on the aircraft's side and this time succour was given. The troops who heard him dug him out and rushed him to a field hospital, whence he was flown to England. For his ordeal, and guts in refusing to give in, he was awarded the DFC.

Later that day the USAAF jettisoned part of their bomb load, a not uncommon procedure when, for example, weather over the target necessitated abandoning an operation or low cloud over base made it perilous to land with a full load of high explosive. On this occasion the B17s and B24s emptied their bomb bays on to the positions of the 51st (Highland) Divison, wounded 300 and killed sixty.

The task of breaking through to Falaise rested on 11 Canadian Corps. Its commander, General C. G. Simmonds, conceived an unconventional plan of attack which is of special significance in the history of air warfare because it involved the first use of strategic bombers in a tactical role. The assault was made at night without the usual artillery barrage that would have warned the enemy that a push was about to start. Instead, Bomber Command opened the battle an hour before midnight on 7 August by bombing the defences on either side of the corridor through which the tanks, and infantry in armoured carriers, would thrust. So revolutionary a tactic could not have been attempted by any other air force in the world. Only the RAF had attained the essential navigational skill and accuracy of target marking.

Working so close to ground forces, the usual procedure for marking targets could not be followed. Immediately, therefore, one was specifically designed for the purpose. Before committing themselves to it, Bomber Command insisted that they must first try it out. The Master Bombers concerned had to ensure that red or green concentrations of marker shells fired from twenty-five pounder guns could be clearly discerned at night. The practice was done on a different part of the line, which was held by the British 1st Corps, and declared satisfactory by the Master Bombers.

The method called for the use of 'Oboe', a radar aid to navigation. The Pathfinder Force's Oboe marker, having located the target by this means, dropped the first marker. The Pathfinders following him dropped more markers. The Master Bomber then went in so low that he could identify the target visually. When he had done so, he ordered 'Bombs away' and the heavies deposited their loads, a total of 4,500 tons.

For the tank crews, the unique necessity to navigate accurately at night presented a vast problem. Half an hour after the first bombs fell the tanks advanced behind the rolling bombardment. To guide them there was a radio directional beam, supplemented by green target indicator shells fired by the artillery, tracer fired by Bofors anti-aircraft guns, searchlights and moonlight. In the event, the tank crews' lack of experience of this kind of mass movement by night, further hindered by the enemy's smoke screen, led to collisions, capsizes and general confusion.

At 1300 hrs the USAAF were let loose on the 11 Corps front, using the same method by daylight as the RAF had used in the dark. The flak was, as usual, thick and nine aircraft were lost. On three of the four target areas the bombing was well concentrated. On the fourth, none of the crews could identify it with certainty and only one aircraft bombed. Out of 678 bombers only 492 did bomb. Twenty-four B17s, carrying 90lb of fragmentation bombs between them, attacked the 3rd Canadian Infantry Division. Their bag was eighty-six killed and 376 wounded, plus seven guns and eighty-three vehicles destroyed.

Nonetheless, the Germans were forced to begin pulling out on 9 August.

On 14 August the RAF was guilty of a rare mistake in identifying the target. Operation Tractable was a massive attack on Falaise, carried out by Canadian 11 Corps. Air support was given by 417 Lancasters, 352 Halifaxes and forty-two Mosquitoes, among which were 300 aircraft from Canadian squadrons. The target was Quesnay Wood, which a strong enemy force was holding. The Pathfinders made a four-mile navigation error and marked the wrong wood. This was duly bombed; 112 Canadians died, 378 were injured, 265 vehicles, thirty guns and two tanks were wiped out.

In this instance there was another grave error that aggravated the tragedy. The Allied ground forces always used yellow smoke flares to indicate their positions to 2nd TAF aircraft. Through inefficient liaison between the RAF and Army Staffs, the Bomber Command aircraft on this operation used their customary yellow smoke target indicators. They should, of course, have been warned not to use this colour, in which event they would have used red. When the bomber crews saw the yellow smoke that their own ground forces released as a safety measure, they naturally thought they were seeing target indicators. When they started to bomb, British anti-aircraft fired at them, but they assumed it was enemy flak and carried on bombing.

The two Staffs' mistake hardly mitigated the fact that it was the misidentification of the target in the first place that caused this classic instance of amicidal fire. Punishments were condign. Two Pathfinder crews were posted to ordinary bomber duties; some squadron and flight commanders were reduced in rank and office and also posted to the bomber main force. All crews involved were suspended from operations within thiry miles of the forward bomb line until they had gained further experience, were reassessed and found satisfactory.

Unusual and unpleasant things were happening to Typhoon pilots, meanwhile. One who baled out was given some protection by a squadron comrade who strafed the nearby flak gunners to prevent them shooting at him. This did not totally deter ground fire, but he landed unwounded – and was immediately captured and tied to a tree. His captors were about to shoot him when a German officer drove up, rescued him and had him put into a lorry that was in convoy. A few minutes later a Typhoon from his squadron strafed the lorry and he was lucky not to be hit.

Another Typhoon pilot had to bale out when his aeroplane caught fire, was burned on the face and arms and hurt his leg against the tailplane. As he hit the ground he saw men waving in apparent friendliness, so, thinking they were French civilians, began limping towards them. He discovered soon enought that they were German soldiers, and presently found himself lying on the floor of an ambulance in which there were four wounded Germans. Red crosses could not always be accepted as genuine. The Germans had taken to putting this marking on lorries carrying troops and war material, to avoid strafing. General Eisenhower had ordered that, despite this, no vehicles showing a red cross was to be attacked. Soldiers, airmen and sailors who actually do the fighting are not inclined to follow orders blindly when they prejudice their own lives and limbs. It was no surprise to the Typhoon pilot when a Spitfire strafed the lorry with its cannon. He was wounded in the legs and shoulders.

On 18 August a plethora of accidental killings among allies occurred, all by RAF and USAAF fighter bombers with rockets, bombs and cannon. More than forty incidents were recorded, causing fifty-one casualties to ground troops and demolishing twenty-five vehicles.

By now 345 (French) Squadron had joined Nos 91 – a British – Squadron and 322 (Dutch) as 141 Wing. They were re-equipped with Spitfire IXs, which had two 20mm cannon and four .303 machine guns, 'an armament more comfortable [than the Spit VA's eight m/gs] for confronting Me109s and FW190s'.

The last week of the month saw the most pitiful of all the episodes during which men were killed and maimed. The Allies had by now advanced beyond Paris, but Le Havre remained in enemy hands. Allied ships at anchor were nightly targets for torpedo bombers, E-boats and midget submarines, while aircraft also sowed mines off the Normandy coast and in the Channel. All day and every day British minesweepers cleared a passage for friendly shipping. Since 18 August one flotilla of six ships had been sweeping a minefield near Le Havre to enable a battleship and two cruisers to shell the port.

On 26 August, during a twenty-four-hour rest, the captain of *HMS Jason*, the flotilla leader, who was a regular officer, was ordered to resume a previous task on the next day – sweeping the Channel between Portsmouth and Arromanches. The importance of sweeping near Le Havre had been given priority over all else, so he was surprised to have these new orders. He sent his navigating officer to the Headquarters Ship to query this sudden and unexpected change. The Staff in the HQ Ship told *Jason*'s navigating officer that the order would again be changed and that the flotilla must resume its unfinished business near Le Havre.

All activity of Allied ships off the French coast had to be notified in advance to the other Services. The HQ Ship should therefore have made an immediate signal to the other Services' Headquarters. One recipient of the signal should have been the Rear-Admiral who was Flag Officer British Assault Area. The Staff Officer responsible for disseminating these signals failed to send any at all.

The flotilla received its new orders next morning before sailing. Only four ships, *Jason*, *Britomart*, *Salamander* and *Hussar*, were able to set off; one was undergoing engine repairs and another had been damaged by a mine. Two trawlers accompanied the four, to lay buoys marking the swept channel. Early in the afternoon *Hussar*'s gear developed a fault and she had to stop sweeping but remained in company with the others. The day was sunny and hot, the off-duty men sunbathed.

At 1330 the ships' companies heard aircraft approaching fast. Streaks of smoke spurted from their wings as rockets hurtled towards the little ships.

They were Typhoons, led by one of the most experienced Typhoon pilots in the RAF. He had flown this type throughout his operational career and by the end of the Normandy campaign was to be recognized as a wing leader of the same outstanding qualities as Johnnie Johnson and 'Kill 'em' Gillam. He also became the highest-scoring Typhoon pilot of the war, with 16½ kills.

J.R. 'Johnny' Baldwin, DFC and bar, who later added a DSO and bar to his decorations and rose to be a group captain, had already enjoyed a highly unusual career. This was not the first time he had been stationed in France, but it was poles apart from his first tour of service there. He had joined the RAF Volunteer Reserve in September, 1939, as an aircraftman on ground duties and was posted to France in 1940. On returning to England he was in a bomb disposal unit before volunteering to fly. When he completed his training in America, he joined 609 Squadron, which was already equipped with Typhoons. In January, 1943, he won a DFC for shooting down three Me109s that were part of a fighter-bomber formation raiding the south coast of England. Later that year he was shot down in flames over the Channel, but unharmed. He scored four more kills before moving to another Typhoon squadron, No 198, as Commanding Officer. He ended that year with two more victories, had a short rest tour as Squadron Leader Tactics at HQ 11 Group of Fighter Command, then was promoted and given command of 146 Wing, 2nd TAF. In this capacity he scored his final three victories. He was shot down and killed in the Korean War.

Johnny Baldwin had been astonished when ordered to take off on this attack against the minesweepers. It was well known that the Royal Navy had been sweeping the Le Havre area for the past week. When airborne he had asked his ground controller for confirmation of the target and was assured that the ships were definitely German. It defied his common sense, so he queried the information twice more while airborne. Each time he was told that the ships he was to attack were definitely not British. When he closed the ships he once more had great doubts, but was left with no option but to carry out his orders.

The Typhoon was armed with four 20mm cannon and eight 60lb rockets or two 1000lb bombs. Perhaps what followed would have been less horrible to be involved in if the aircraft were carrying bombs on this operation. Rockets were easier to aim and their destructive power was devastating and hideous to behold for anyone who did not regard working in an abbatoir as a pleasant occupation.

Immediately the Typhoons opened fire, *Jason* reported the fact by wireless to her Headquarters. Two minutes later her captain saw that two minesweepers had been hit and were listing heavily. The fighters swept round for a second run and *Jason* fired the correct recognition signals. The reply was a burst of cannon shells. Rockets had already set *Salamander* alight and *Britomart* and *Hussar* were also burning. One of the trawlers, Colsay, had stopped. *Jason* had returned the attackers' fire with her two Oerlikons and now reported to Headquarters that the burning vessels were in danger of sinking.

The Typhoons came in for a second run and, eleven minutes after their first salvoes, they flew away.

Two of the burning ships were sinking and the third was listing badly. Men, some of them wounded, were in the water among wreckage and corpses. One sweeper sent her motor launch to pick up survivors, but she had been holed by cannon shells and sank after a few men had been hauled aboard.

Another sweeper capsized before going down. Fourteen of her officers and ratings had been killed and more than seventy wounded. Another went down by the stern. Fifty-three of her officers and ratings died and thirty-nine were wounded.

About a quarter of an hour after the attack began, an RAF air/ sea rescue high speed launch arrived and began taking surivivors from the water. She was presently joined by two minesweepers. One trawler had suffered six casualties but was able to help with the rescue work.

Altogether, seventy-eight of all ranks were killed and 149 wounded.

The butchery at Falaise was, in a different way, as distressing an infliction on the fighter and fighter bomber pilots as it was on the enemy. No one but a psychopath can be other than revolted by having to kill and mutilate fellow beings on the scale that this had to be done during those days. Fifty years after the orgy of wholesale destruction, there are still pilots who decline to reminisce about it.

Voltaire did not have a battlefield in mind when he wrote the following lines, nor is the passion that is aroused in combat of the kind on which he reflected; but to do one's duty against an enemy who has set out to subjugate the world is a great work and it often must be done in a seeming frenzy. The quotation seems relevant.

'Il faut qu'il y ait des moments tranquilles dans les grands ouvrages, comme dans la vie après les instants de passions, mais non pas des moments de dégoût.'

'There ought to be moments of tranquillity in great works, as in life after the experience of passion, but not moments of disgust.'

Air Vice Marshal J. E. J. Johnson, CB, CBE, DSO and two bars, DFC and bar is not only a famous warrior but also posessor of a generously humane spirit. General Galland is a friend of his and forty-odd years after the war he was elected an honorary member of the German Fighter Pilots' Association – a unique compliment. In his view, the right and proper place for fighter pilots to operate is high above the earth and against their own kind. In his book *Wing Leader*, published twelve years after Falaise, he wrote that, a few days after the fighting had moved on from there, the *Luftwaffe*, now operating from bases near Paris, was putting up a fighter screen over the Seine to cover the retreating ground forces from further air attack. It was suggested that if two squadrons of his wing were to patrol well to the south of Paris and then approach the Seine from the east (up sun), they might have some luck.

In his words, 'It would be a pleasant change to operate in our true rôle after the carnage of Falaise. Beating up the German Army was part of our job, but it was a poor substitute for the clean, exhilarating thrill of the dogfight.'

He accordingly took 441 and 443 Squadrons hunting. Despite the enemy's penury of serviceable aircraft, fuel and pilots, they met sixty-plus Me109s and FW190s of which they shot down twelve. Johnny Johnson bagged two of them.

16

SOME *LUFTWAFFE* EXPERIENCES
AND VIEWS

After the Allies broke through the German line at Falaise, mollifying reports of the *Luftwaffe's* air strength were presented to Hitler by his frightened toadies.

General Galland contemptuously condemned this practice and quotes the figures for one day; '250 fighter and 180 fighter bomber sorties; the facts do not emerge from the very detailed and factually indisputable battle reports. Fifty-seven lost, not even fifteen per cent! But it did not say in these reports that on the same day twenty-seven aircraft were burned out on airfield X; that on the landing strip, Y Squadron was annihilated by enemy fighter bombers while taking off; that Z Squadron lost fifty per cent of its strength transferring from one base to another [shot down by Allied fighters]. Who [in the High Command] was interested in the daily loss of materiel and men? Where was the *Luftwaffe*? Who cared that the daily sorties of 430 aircraft had no other operative effect than for the fighter bombers and fighters to be routed by the enemy?'

He goes on to say that during his visits to units at the front he realized the disproportion between the effort and the result of the German Air Force's actions.

German technical officers as well as fighter pilots who remember the crucial period 7 to 16 August recall it as a time of desperation and despair. One captain has said, 'Unfortunately it was plainly seen from the first hours of the invasion that there was no clear leadership. Plans were constantly changed, the consequence of which was that owing to misinformation our ground organization would turn up at the wrong airfield. Of the Maquis, during the early days, there was little sign. However, our maintenance crews were subjected to heavy attacks along the roads by fighter bombers, so that they were split up and out of touch with each other. As our last destination we were told to go to the Le Mans airfield. I arrived there with my vehicles to find that some of our transport had been lost on the way. Conditions were catastrophic. A fighter *Gruppe* had been transferred to Le Mans from Germany. Of some twenty-five machines, only four were serviceable. The rest had either lost their way or been shot down in flames. On the edge of the airfield lay more burned out Ju52s that had brought ground personnel. There was no hope at all of flying any sorties. Low level attacks had done their work. The alarm that called pilots to take off sounded no more, while Marauders cruised overhead.

'Finally, in the general confusion we received the information that our *Gruppe* must move to Guyancourt. The next day we witnessed a depressing event. On a stretch of road several kilometres long and totally without shelter, we encountered a column of about twenty-five lorries carrying twenty-one centimetre mortars straight from the factory. Before our eyes, four Mustangs pounced on them. After a quarter of an hour and seven attacks, no more than three or four of these vehicles were left. The rest remained at hundred-metre intervals, in flames. Later the same scene was repeated several times on a smaller scale. Two days later a *Schwärm*[section of four] of fighters was made available for the protection of supply routes.'

The distinguished JG26 was leading a peripatetic existence. The Headquarters and I JG26, its No 1 *Gruppe*, were at Boissy le Bois, on 29 July they were at Mesnuls, on 16 August back at Boissy. On 21 August I JG26 was at Vitry and on 22 August the HQ was at Valenciennes. On 20 July II JG26 had gone to Germany for a rest. It returned to Guyancourt on 12 August but had to leave at once for St Quentin and Mons. III JG26 stayed near Villacoublay until the end of August, then withdrew to Rosières and Chièvres.

This *Gruppe* was typical of all such fighter formations and its losses can be taken as a fair indication of the odds against it after D-Day. In 1943 total losses, not including the wounded, were 167 air and ground personnel. Between 1 January and 5 June, 1944, it lost 114; 106 pilots killed in action, in accidents and missing, and eight ground crew. From 6 June to 31 December, 1944, the total losses were 199; 186 pilots and 13 ground crew.

17

BEYOND NORMANDY

After Falaise the road to Berlin awaited. The period from D-Day to the end of August was decisive. Another eight months of fighting lay ahead, as tough as during those first twelve weeks, but ultimate victory had already been assured. It is worth moving on to consider later operations in order to put the early ones in perspective and understand the contribution they made to wearing down the enemy land force as well as the air force.

R. E. G. Sheward, known as Ronnie, was one of several Britons resident in Argentina who returned to England, where, like him, many of them had been educated, to volunteer for the RAF. In the Service he was addressed variously as Shewy or Bentos – the last because bully beef tins bore this Argentinian place name as their source of origin.

On 1 November, 1944, he was posted from England to 266 (Rhodesia) Squadron in 2nd TAF at Antwerp. His first sorties were to rocket railway trucks, enemy-occupied buildings, road and rail bridges in Flanders and Holland. Eighteen days after joining the squadron he was given command of 'A' Flight. Six days later he moved to 263 Squadron as 'B' Flight commander.

He has revealed an astonishing item of information. 'I have recently found out from a friend who was with Army Intelligence in Brussels at the time that the electricity company in Holland had a direct line from the occupied north part of Holland to the south part, which had been liberated, without the Germans ever finding out. So we were receiving direct requests over the telephone line giving us full details of our target.'

On the day after he joined his new squadron one such request was to be complied with; they had been asked to destroy the Gestapo Headquarters in Amsterdam, where incriminating records about members of the Resistance were kept. Their lives would be forfeit if these were not destroyed. The RAF warned the Dutch that there were bound to be civilian casualties. The reply came that this was understood and acceptable. The strike had to be made between 1230 and 1330, when the children from a nearby school would have gone home to lunch and 'Gestapo personnel would be eating their sauerkraut behind the Gestapo HQ,' says Ronnie Sheward.

It was a wing effort, led by Group Captain D. E. Gillam, DSO and two bars, DFC and bar, known as 'Kill 'em' Gillam and regarded by many as the greatest ground-attack expert of all. He had fought in the Battle of Britain, in which he made eight kills, to which in time one and a half were added. Douglas Bader described him as 'the unrivalled maestro of the low-level attack technique'.

Four Typhoons of 263 Squadron took part, each carrying two 1,000lb bombs, flown by the CO, Squadron Leader Rutter, DFC, who had also been in the Battle of Britain, Flight Lieutenant Sheward and two Canadians, Flying Officers Hamilton and Woodward. Rutter took his pilots in first, 'low and fast with masterly navigation. It went like a treat, our eight bombs went right through the front of the building,' says Sheward. 'If you keep low enough, fly straight at the target and press the tit just before the leading edge of your wing disappears from sight, you can't miss. The rest of the wing were attacking other targets, such as flak positions, and some were detailed to dive rocket with incendiaries, which resulted in a good burn up. Success! The building was in ruins and Dutch houses adjacent undamaged.'

Three days after the Amsterdam operation the wing mounted a similar attack against the Gestapo HQ in Rotterdam, on which Sheward led eight aircraft of his squadron whose task this time was anti-flak. They made two attacks on barges and gun positions in the dock area.

Casualties on ground attack operations were heavy. His logbook records; 24 December, 'Flight Lieutenant Unwin shot down by flak. Missing.' 26 December, 'Flight Lieutenant Turner killed.' 27 December, 'Pilot Officer Scott-Edie and Flight Sergeant Green 266 [Squadron] shot down by 60-plus Me109s and FW190s. Scott-Edie POW, Green killed.'

The next few entries show strikes against barges, and a rocket attack that destroyed a German observation post on which he was hit by flak – of which there was always ample.

On 1 January, 1945, Squadron Leader Rutter was posted on rest and Squadron Leader Rumbold DFC took over from him. The next day Rumbold was on leave, so Flight Lieutenant Sheward, senior flight commander, was to lead eight aircraft armed with rockets on Army support. The whole countryside was under snow. Shortly before they were due to take off, the noise of aircraft was heard. Eight FW190s and eight Me109s appeared, flying quite slowly, straight and level, and 'strafed a few of our aircraft but put up a very poor show and were being shot at by our AA guns. I yelled "Weave, you stupid bastards, weave!" Recce Mustangs got two and AA claimed nine.' This inept performance by the German pilots was evidence of the general poor quality of the enemy's fighter arm since its heavy casualties in the spring and early summer.

Friendly aircraft could unwittingly prove more dangerous than enemy. On 5 January; 'Taxied out to lead eight aircraft on request from the Army, to make a recce to see how strong the enemy was, when I saw a Typhoon flying over our heads trying to dislodge a bomb which was stuck. It came off, exploded and damaged four of my aircraft, which were unable to take off. Flying Control called me to abandon mission. I felt I couldn't let the Army down, so after finding out that four of us were OK, I led the remaining aircraft and we strafed houses and roads where Army requested, with good results.'

In turn, all squadrons were sent home for leave and a short rest. On 13 January he led all eighteen aircraft of 263 to Fairwood

Common via Tangmere, for rest and arms practice. On 7 February they took off for Antwerp via Manston. Sheward was told that he would receive further orders *en route*, which rather dismayed him 'in case my R/T [radio telephone] packed up.' When the order came it was to divert to Gilze Rijzen. There, two further surprises awaited him and his pilots. The group captain in command told them he would have their aeroplanes bombed up and they must attack railway lines west of Utrecht, on their way to a new base, B89.

All anyone can do in a war is try to adjust his life in a constantly changing frame. Some of the vagaries of active service produce situations that are as droll as they are hazardous. On 20 February Flight Lieutenant Sheward took three of his pilots in a jeep to Goch, where they found that soldiers were hiding in the doorways of shops, so he stopped to ask the form. 'I wouldn't go much further, mate, keen sniper up the other end – nasty,' he was told. He had driven a few yards to turn round when small arms fire and all the other sounds of a brisk gunfight close at hand sent the pilots leaping from the jeep to dash into a shop. 'It was full of white boxes with opera hats in them. We each selected our own size and when things had calmed down came out suitably hatted, much to the Army's amusement. I still have mine in good condition.' An episode that agreeably encapsulates the traditional RAF fighter pilots' attitude to life.

The ensuing days' work comprised the usual succession of rocket or bombing attacks on railway lines, roads, barges and buildings occupied by the enemy.

On 7 March he was promoted to squadron leader and returned to 266 as Squadron Commander.

On 19 March the squadron attacked a target of particular importance, which was the subject of mention in the Press. The objective was a tank and motor transport repair depot at Doetinchem. The newspaper paragraph read, 'A smashing blow was struck during the afternoon at the enemy ability to equip and refit armoured fighting vehicles for the big battles that cannot be long delayed on the British sector of the Western Front. A repair depot near Emmerich capable of dealing with over 500 tanks and other fighting vehicles was wrecked by Typhoons. A reconnaissance pilot said, "It was a miniature Falaise. I don't think one vehicle escaped".' Ronnie Sheward's comment is, 'Pushing it a bit. Not nearly so dangerous as Falaise.'

On 19 March Squadron Leader Sheward led the wing in a strike against a factory at Doetinchem, on which Wing Commander Johnny Deal and Group Captain Wells also flew.

On 24 March the squadron operated in support of airborne landings in the Wesel area. He says, 'During the airborne landings our job was to silence the flak gun batteries.' They operated in pairs. 'One aircraft would draw the fire while the other stayed up, spotted the flashes and dived quickly. We would then change places. An ideal pastime for anyone who was tired of living.'

His entry for 8 May, 1945, is; 'War in Europe terminated and three of my pilots were liberated. They'd had a rotten time, beaten up and paraded about. Flying Officers Dodd Shepherd and Scott-Edie. The latter, whose hair was quite black when shot down, was now totally white.'

Squadron Leader R. E. G. Sheward's war record earned him a well deserved Distinguished Flying Cross.

Pilot Officer John Shellard (later Flight Lieutenant) was also a pilot on 263 Squadron – one of five squadrons in 146 Wing. He had arrived at B3 airfield on 6 August, 1944.

The main trouble about attacks, he says, was the difficulty in assessing results. He quotes from his logbook: 'Attack on red smoke pinpointing troops'. The flying time on the sortie was thiry-five minutes, which is an indication of how near the airfield was to the front line. Often, eight aircraft would take off together and return in pairs, having split up to attack various targets.

As an example of a typical attack, he cites an armed reconnaissance over a large area that lasted an hour. The section found some trucks, with tanks lined nose to tail under some trees, which they attacked in a thirty-degree dive. He fired his rockets in pairs 'as did the other three Tiffies (I think)'. When they came round again at low level three tanks were on fire, so they 'cannoned the trucks and wreckage before pulling up to 1000ft to return to base'.

The wing was commanded by Wing Commander J. R. Baldwin. Under his leadership, John Shellard took part in an attack by the whole wing on 16 August, against a château at Bernay that was a German headquarters. No 263 was the last squadron to go in, by which time smoke obscured most of the target. Abruptly it cleared enough to reveal a small building in the courtyard. Shellard chose it as his aiming point and fired a salvo – all eight rockets – before re-forming. At briefing, Baldwin asked who had been the last man in 263 to fire.

'I was, sir.'

'Did you see the result?'

'No, I was too busy watching where I was going.' A major concern when sixty aeroplanes were milling around in a small airspace.

'Pity. You blew the damn place up.'

The small building, its assailant reasonably concluded, 'must have been an ammo store.'

Weeks and months rolled by, the enemy retreated. Troops, tanks, vehicles of every sort, rolling stock, locomotives, railway track, buildings of all kinds, bridges, barges, a paddle steamer on the Seine, were left mangled in the squadron's path.

The war would be over in a few weeks. The squadron flew three times on a day memorable for its variety and the scale of one of its tasks.

It began with an attack on a fortified farm house on the German side of the Rhine, which was being used as a SS headquarters, led by the Commanding Officer, Squadron Leader R. E. G. Sheward; 'and the whole thing went like a practice drill. We all had direct hits with salvoes of R/P [rocket projectiles], leaving the place wrecked'. They were unaware that a photo recce Mosquito was 15,000ft overhead, recording the event.

The next item on the programme was very different. The US 101st Airborne Division was to make the bridgehead that would lead to the invasion of Germany in the north of the battlefront. The wing was patrolled at 1,000ft to 'take out any flak we could see'. General Montgomery had ordered 'an area of a couple of square miles' selected for the drop and the Rhine crossing to be 'saturated with artillery fire for a few hours beforehand.' J. W. Shellard looks back on it with evident awe. 'Imagine hundreds of aircraft, Liberators, Dakotas, Typhoons, gliders etc all in a couple or so square miles and all at roughly the same height, and all in a thick cloud of grey/brown murk thrown up by the artillery, mortars and general conflagration. All we could feel was the prop wash from aircraft we couldn't see and which suddenly appeared in front somewhere, but we never saw flak! There were "holes" briefly now and again, but it was advisable to keep one's eyes looking forward. When we eventually came out of the "cloud" to return to base, the amazing thing was that our lot were all in the same piece of sky.

'Later that day I flew again on an armed recce, but I can't remember the details of that one.'

On 25 August he was in an attack that sank a paddle steamer and several other attacks on bridges across the Seine, over which the Germans were retreating.

The last major event of his war was 'the shooting down of the last German fighter to be shot down by Tiffies in WW2'. The three other pilots who took part were Flight Lieutenant Gus Fowler, Pilot Officer David Morgan and Warrant Officer Jock Barrie. Their mission was 'train busting on the German/Danish border'. They found a train, but after making their attack Morgan called on the R/T to say that he was making a forced landing. Fowler and Shellard were still in the dive when Barrie's voice warned that 'two Me262 jets were attempting a bounce, having broken through the cloud base at approximately 6000ft. The leading 262 overshot and Jock gave him a long burst before turning to cover David. The E/A [enemy aircraft] turned again and Gus was able to fire and then it was my turn. After my shots I could see he was on fire, so pulled the nose up and gave the No 2 E/A a burst before turning to watch the first 262 go down. Gus also gave the No 2 a burst, but it was not interested in a scrap, had turned up the wicks and headed for the clouds, so that our shots at him were from very long range. Later, when David had been released [from captivity] he told me that he had been taken to the mess of the 262 squadron and the man we shot down had over 60 victories.'

The German pilot thought that David Morgan had got the leader and he, the German No 2, had then got Morgan. 'David did not know whether he had suffered flak damage or engine failure, but knew that he hadn't fired at any E/A or had been shot at. He also said that he was not in a position to argue'!

When the other three pilots made their combat reports, the conclusion was that David Morgan had been hit by flak from the train. The credit for the destruction of the Me262 was shared equally between his companions.

18

ROCKET AND FIGHTER-BOMBING ATTACK TECHNIQUES

Wing Commander (now Air Vice Marshal) 'Johnnie' Johnson has given a succint description of dive bombing as done by fighter bombers. The Spitfire IX could carry two 500 pounders. The pilot put his aircraft into a steep dive, aimed at the target and released his bombs at about the same time as he pulled out of his dive. It is that 'about' which made the operation interesting. Each pilot had to make his own judgment. The bombs did not follow the same line of flight as the aeroplane's, so if the pilot aimed directly at the target, they fell short. He also had to make allowance for the wind. Some counted to three before letting their bombs go, others to four, some released them as the target passed through a certain portion of the gunsight. Sometimes, when bombing from fairly high, he half-rolled into a dive and released his bombs when the target disappeared from view under the wing.

There were other ways. In 1942 126 Squadron, based in Malta, had devised its own bomb rack to carry one 250lb bomb under the fuselage of its Spitfire Vs. With these it first dive-bombed targets in Sicily in September that year. The method was to approach over the sea at less than 50ft, climb steeply to 4,000ft when ten miles offshore, dive at an angle of between twenty-five and forty degrees, according to the position of the target, release the bomb half way down, hold the dive almost to ground level and return to base skimming the sea.

By the time the Allies invaded Italy, on 10 July, 1943, some

Spitfire Vs were fitted with two racks, each carrying a 250lb bomb. There were two standard bombing techniques. One was to approach the target at between 18,000ft and 20,000ft and, when dead overhead, to stall turn through 180 degrees before diving vertically and releasing the bombs at 10,000ft. This procedure was highly accurate but vulnerable to both heavy and light flak.

Another one was to approach the target in V formation, in threes, so that it lay on a flank. When nearing the target, the pilots watched their port or starboard wing, according to the side on which the target was, steering so that it appeared between the wingtip and the cannon that protruded from the wing about nine feet inboard. The target then disappeared briefly, obscured by the wing, and reappeared behind the trailing edge. At that moment they turned towards it, went into a 75 degree dive and released their bombs at 13,000ft, which was above the light and medium flak, and immediately pulled up to start dodging the heavy flak. That was also accurate, but both techniques were superseded by a third.

This had originally been intended for bombing airfields but was equally effective against buildings, railway yards, barracks and groups of aircraft or a tank lager, but not against scattered tanks or other small objectives. It was necessary to trim the aircraft nose-heavy before starting the dive, because there would not be time to do it later. Again, the formation flew in Vs of three, in two flights of six aircraft, the flights separated by a mile. At 20,000ft they formed echelon starboard – a line slanting back on the leader's right. What followed was a beautiful, rhythmic pattern; in concert, they winged over and pulled through into a shallow dive, the Spitfires making a lovely picture when their pointed wings and slim bellies, painted duck-egg blue, flicked over. They held the dive to 18,000ft and when the outer limit of the target area came in sight just under his port wing root, the leader half-rolled to the left and pulled through into a vertical dive. By this manoeuvre each section was now in echelon port. Using their reflector gunsights, they released their bombs at 10,000ft, by which time their indicated air speed was

450 mph. At 8,000ft they eased out but continued diving steeply to treetop height and left the target area skimming the trees and ground so closely that it was impossible for flak or machine guns to hit them.

Rocket firing demanded experience and skill. That gallant Belgian, Raymond Lallemant, who ended his Service career as a lieutenant-colonel in the Belgian Air Force, was a brilliant exponent of the best technique. Having served as a sergeant pilot in 609 Squadron from July, 1941, in which he was later commissioned, he did a second tour as a flight commander in 198 before returning to 609 as Commanding Officer in mid-1944. He had converted to Typhoons in early 1942 and, between his first and second operational tours, spent six months as a production test pilot at Napier's, who made the engines.

Typhoons had no elaborate gunsight. 'The best we had,' he says, 'was a modification of the standard sight made by Roland Beamont when he commanded 609.'

Most rockets struck short of the target, owing to pilot inexperience and enemy anti-aircraft fire. He explains, 'We had to be very low to escape the accurate German flak. That led to fear of collision with obstacles on the ground. Don't think the German tanks were silly enough to park in the middle of a field – they knew about camouflage!

'I must admit that most of my own lucky shots were the result of a last check in the gunsight – split seconds take you closer to your target very swiftly in a diving Typhoon.' When he hit the target it was through guts and accuracy, not luck. He 'became involved in a sharp argument' with Wing Commander Dring, the Wing Leader, 'over my practice of making a pass at low level before firing, in order to pick out the tanks from the "soft-skinned" vehicles.' Dring told him that this gave the flak a double chance to shoot the aircraft down, 'but I considered it essential'.

Caution must not be allowed to enter into it, he maintained. 'The real point was to trace the tanks and kill them before they could run for shelter. When they were in the open a vertical dive was best, but not all pilots could put their aircraft into such a position, since one always gains the impression within the aircraft that the dive is steeper than is really the case.' What he means, politely, is that not everyone can steel himself to hurtle earthwards vertically at several hundred miles an hour and pull out before he slams into the ground, all within a few seconds. The method of checking that they were in the right attitude which he recommended to his pilots sounds draconian; 'I advised them to do a roll during the dive, since in a shallow dive they would feel uncomfortable when the aircraft was on its back; in a vertical dive no such gravity pull would be experienced'. Not nearly as uncomfortable as making your heavy aeroplane rotate about its longitudinal axis and taking up a few of the seconds between life and death, but they did it.

The eight sixty-pound rockets and their rails under the wings not only added weight but also had an adverse aerodynamic effect. Pilots therefore rid themselves of the missiles as soon as possible before going on to find targets vulnerable to their four 20mm cannon. When a vertical diving attack was not practical, they went into a shallow dive from a height between three hundred and five hundred feet, fired from a range of five hundred yards and immediately climbed away, which allowed them four or five seconds to gain a height at which they would be safe from splinters when the rockets exploded.

What Group Captain Denys Gillam, whom Group Captain Sir Douglas Bader regarded as the greatest of all ground attack pilots and leaders, had to say about attacking ships was relevant to all targets at sea or on the ground that were strongly protected by flak. Group Captain Bader records that, 'It was an expensive business'. He reckoned that 615 Squadron lost about fifty Hurricanes and fifteen to twenty pilots during its ten weeks at Manston. The German convoys were escorted sometimes by as many as eight flak ships, which were specially built and heavily armed for anti-aircraft duties. Their fire power was considerable and accurate against low-flying attackers who needed to fly straight on the run-in to the target, and could only jink in evasive action as they went away.

This is the account that Gillam gave him. 'We approached the target in two sections of four, each section in line abreast, alongside each other; the section leaders were in the middle of this formation of eight. At the right distance from the target, the two leaders throttled back, thus allowing the outside men to get ahead. Then all eight Hurricanes pulled up and dived on the target with cannons (sic) and machine guns. As soon as we passed over it, we were down on the water and jinking away. Out of range, we would re-form and have a go from a different direction.

'The cast-iron rule was that one Hurricane or even one section of four should never attack alone. By our method, we dispersed the flak and confused the enemy gunners.'

Apart from the obvious fact that a cannon shell did not have the destructive power of a rocket with a 50lb explosive head, rockets had another advantage over guns; they were self-propelling, so there was no equal and opposite reaction to slow the aircraft when they were released. The recoil of four 20mm cannon reduced the speed of an aeroplanne by some 40 mph.

19

THE TYPHOON

The Spitfire was a sweet-natured lady and its Rolls Royce Merlin engine the equivalent in engineering terms of a Stradivarius in the world of music. The Typhoon was a heavy-weight bruiser and its Napier Sabre engine was, to follow the metaphor, a bassoon capable of blowing a raspberry when its player expected a decently euphonious note. The early production Typhoons sometimes suffered a structural failure, particularly when pulling out of a steep dive, which caused the tail unit to break off. This was rectified, but several pilots were killed in the interim. The sleeve-valve Sabre engine had been put into service before the deficiencies always shown by new designs had been detected and rectified. By the time these aeroplanes reached the squadrons that were to form an indispensable part of 2nd TAF, the necessary improvements had been made; but the engine still caused some problems.

To start, it had to be carefully primed, taking into account whether it was cold or still warm after recent use. The pilot pushed a button that fired a Koffmann cartridge, which injected gas under high pressure into one cylinder, whose piston set the crankshaft in motion. After two or three revolutions, a matter of a split second, the engine should catch and the propeller start to turn immediately after the cartridge exploded. If it did not start at the first attempt, there was a danger of fire in the air intake. Two men with extinguishers stood ready. Failure to start also meant a leak of gas into the cockpit, so the pilots always fastened their oxygen masks as soon as they entered the cockpit.

If three attempts did not succeed, the airscrew was turned manually to pump the gas out and the starting procedure was repeated. However, failure to start was rare among experienced pilots and ground crews.

Like the Spitfire, the Typhoon had a long nose that prevented its pilot looking straight ahead when taxiing, so he had to swerve from side to side. With the Beaufighter and some other types, the Typhoon shared a tendency to swing violently to the left when accelerating on take-off, particulary when the tail rose from the ground. Numerous Beaufighters and Typhoons had crashed owing to this characteristic that had been inherent in aeroplanes since the Sopwith Camel in 1917, the most successful single-seat fighter of the Great War. The powerful tug to the left could be scary at first, but it was not an aberration, it was a logical fact of dynamics, merely caused by torque and countered by applying right rudder with appropriate force.

The crops on acres of ground had to be ripped up, grass, bushes and trees torn from the soil, to make room for airfields. The resulting dust that rose from the bare, dry earth was a constant plague of the Normandy air strips and another reason for pilots to fasten their oxygen masks. The obvious risks of taking off in zero visibility have already been mentioned, but the pilots would soon be clear of the choking, blinding miasma. The ground crews had no relief until the dust settled – if there was time before more take-offs and landings. They tied scarves over their mouths and noses and protected their eyes with anti-gas goggles.

The dust permeated the engines. Filters had been used in the desert and now they were needed again. Some squadrons were able to fit them on site, others flew back to England to have it done. It also clogged the cannon and caused stoppages, unless every drop of oil was wiped off.

20

THE DOCTRINE OF
AIR SUPERIORITY

The essence of the Overlord plan was to ensure air superiority, which was achieved. It could not have been without the conversion of the Generals to a reversal of their attitude at the outbreak of war and consequent defeat of the British Expeditionary Force in 1940. Fortunately four intelligent Air Officers Commanding in North Africa and Italy – Air Marshal Sir Arthur Longmore, Air Commodore Raymond Collishaw, Air Vice Marshal Arthur Coningham and Air Vice Marshal Harry Broadhurst – and four equally perceptive and co-operative General Officers Commanding – Sir Archibald Wavell, Sir Claude Auchinlech, Sir Harold Alexander and Sir Bernard Montgomery – produced close Army-RAF co-operation. The system of battleground air support devised in the Western Desert and Italy transformed tactics and strategy and was the progenitor of the coming victory in the France and Germany Campaign.

Had this momentous change in the mentality of Britain's most senior Army officers come about in 1918, and if the anti-militaristic attitude of successive British Govermnents had not withered and crippled the country's armed forces, defeat in the 1940 Battle of France could have been avoided. The lesson was plain at the end of the First World War: its last eleven months had shown that the dominance of the Royal Flying Corps (which, combined with the Royal Naval Air Service, became the Royal Air Force on 1 April, 1918) was the key to victory. The Field Marshals and Generals had failed to understand that it is only air power that can win freedom of action over enemy territory. By 1939 the world's air forces had two new resources that were not fully appreciated: high speed and the ability to operate at great altitude – which made it possible to carry out photographic reconaissance unobserved by the enemy.

The basic fact that the land commanders had to learn was that air power does not concern air operations only: it is the power to establish air superiority applied to conquest. The side that fails to gain air superiority over the vital area cannot frustrate the enemy's strategy or tactics or influence decisively the land battle to win and hold ground.

By 1943, when the planning of the invasion of Normandy began, the necessary wisdom had at last penetrated the military brains. The conduct of Operation Overlord and the campaign leading to Berlin that would follow was bound to end in victory – given the excellent fighting qualities of the Allied forces.

It was fortunate that the Germans, despite the devastating use of the *Luftwaffe* in its *Blitzkrieg* role, were still ignorant of the fact that attrition no longer wins a war. Instead, as Air Marshal Sir Victor Goddard puts it, 'The enemy's eyes must first be put out', then his air force defeated, if victory on land is to be won.

By 1944 the campaigns that had preceded the assault on France, the Low Countries and, finally, Germany itself enabled the Allies to draw conclusions that were relevant to the battles that began with the Normandy landings. Twelve days after D-Day, Air Marshal Sir John Slessor, Commander-in-Chief RAF Mediterranean and Deputy C-in-C Allied Air Forces Mediterranean, wrote the following succint and perceptive appreciation, The Effect of Air Power in a Land Offensive.

The preamble, numbered 1, was followed by:-

2   It may clear the issue to mention first the things that air power cannot be expected to do in a land campaign of this nature:

(a) It cannot by itself defeat a highly organized and disciplined army, even when that army is virtually without air support of its own. The German will fight defensively without air support or cover, and does not become demoralized by constant air attack against his communications and back areas. The heaviest and most concentrated air bombardment of organized defensive positions cannot be relied upon to obliterate resistance and enable our land forces to advance without loss.

(b) It cannot by itself enforce a withdrawal by drying up the flow of essential supplies. The German's efficient Q [Quartermaster] organization, his policy of living on the country regardless of the interests of the inhabitants, and his extreme frugality and hardiness result in an unsurpassed capacity to maintain his stocks in apparently impossible circumstances at the essential minimum, in circumstances when he is not being forced to expend ammunition, fuel, vehicles, engineer stores, etc at a high rate.

(c) It cannot entirely prevent the movement of strategic reserves from one part of the front to another, or of forward troops to fresh positions in rear.

(d) In short, it cannot absolutely isolate the battlefield from enemy supply or reinforcement.

(e) It cannot absolutely guarantee the immunity either of our forward formations or back areas, port installations, base depots, airfields, convoys at sea, etc against the occasional air attack or reconnaissance.

3 What it can do, and has done in the present battle which, it must be remembered, began with the preliminary air offensive on about March 15, is to make it impossible for the most highly organized and disciplined army to offer prolonged resistance to a determined offensive on the ground – even in country almost ideally suited for defence; it can turn an orderly retreat into a rout; and virtually eliminate an entire army as an effective fighting force.

The converse of 2(a) is equally true. An army by itself cannot, in modern warfare, defeat a highly organized and disciplined army on the defensive. The power of the defence on land has not been overcome by the tank or by improved artillery technique, but by air power. It is doubtful whether anyone could be found to deny that, if there had been no Air Force on either side, the German Army could have made the invasion of Italy impossible except at a cost in national effort and human life which the Allies would have been unwilling to face.

What this meant in the context of the Normandy landings and the defeat of the enemy in the fighting all the way to Berlin was that battlefield air support had been brought to as close to perfection as was contemporaneously possible.

The result was that the enemy soon feared the Typhoons more than any other attacker from the air or on the ground. The time came when German troops, who had never lacked bravery or discipline, would hasten out of their tanks when they saw Typhoons approaching. It was either that or be roasted alive when rockets or bombs set the tank on fire or blew it up.

21

THE SYSTEM OF
CLOSE AIR SUPPORT
FOR THE GROUND FORCES

The Germans felt the effects of Allied air supremacy far beyond the battlefield. It dictated their strategy and tactics, interfered with the construction of their defences along the French coast, reduced the output of factories that built every sort of military equipment, played havoc with logistics and caused deep psychological damage, of which the gravest was the weakening of morale.

The prime instrument of air supremacy after D–Day was the organization by which the land force's requests for help from ground attack fighters could be met within a few minutes. The Rover Control system was a product of the land/air liaison originated in North Africa. A South African fighter bomber pilot, David Heysham, conceived it when he was Group Captain Operations at Desert Air Force Headquarters in Italy. It was used for the first time on 23 October, 1943, in Italy.

In the Western Desert lack of aircraft during the first twelve months of the fighting that had begun in June, 1940, had limited the RAF's support for the Army to bombing. During the early battles in 1941, Air Commodore Collishaw, DSO, OBE, DSC, DFC, one of the greatest fighter leaders of the First World War, was Air Officer Commanding 204 Group. This formation was the embryo that became Desert Air Force, and Collishaw, whose shrewdness has never had sufficient recognition, was its begetter. In May and June, 1941, when the land forces commander,

Brigadier Gott, asked him to concentrate his attention on the German and Italian tanks, Collishaw explained why this would be a waste of petrol, engine hours, aircraft and lives. The Italians' intensive bombing of British armour had done little damage, which proved that tanks were difficult targets because they were small, mobile and able to shoot back at low flying aeroplanes. Enemy tank lagers were well defended by anti-aircraft and so were lorry parks. The most useful contribution the air force could make was for light bombers to machine gun, and drop anti-personnel bombs on, petrol tankers and the big lorries that carried troops. Deprived of petrol, the tanks, armoured cars and motor transport would be halted.

Whatever the policy, it could never be fully effective until communications were improved. The Army provided little information, the blame for which lay in two causes. One was the failure of the ground to follow the agreed signalling procedure. Aircraft would send the correct signals and receive no response – sometimes because the recipients did not know the letters of the day. The other was the atmospheric conditions, which distorted or shortened the range of wireless and often left Army HQ unaware of where their units were.

In September, 1941, an Air Support Directive was issued that defined direct and indirect support. The first was intended to have an immediate effect on current land or sea operations by impeding the enemy's land and air offensive and by destroying the enemy ground forces. Close support was defined as direct offensive support in close proximity to own forward troops. Indirect air support was that given to land or sea forces against objectives other than enemy forces engaged in the tactical battle, but which had an effect on ground forces, although not an immediate one.

This was followed by the formation of joint RAF-Army Air Support Control centres, to be known as ASC, in each army corps and armoured division. The ASCs would keep in touch with brigades through a mobile wireless telegraphy tentacle. A brigade would pass requests for air support by Morse to its ASC, which would evaluate it. If the ASC granted the request, it would notify a Rear Air Support Link (RASL) by radio telephone, which would pass the message on to the airfield by radio telephone. By this means brigades' wireless telegraphy requests should be swiftly received, evaluated and acted on. Every brigade would have a RAF Forward Air Support Link (FASL) to control supporting aircraft by R/T and receive reports.

Air Vice Marshal Coningham had taken over from Collishaw in July. He set up the ASC in his own HQ, which he had established adjacent to that of Lieutenant-General Sir Alan Coningham, the new commander of the land force which, in September, was named Eighth Army.

This orchestration of endeavour, though vigorous, did not at first prove to be as baleful to the enemy as its instigators expected. The conditions in which the new procedure was put into practice were as unfavourable as those confronting an understudy pitched into the first night of a West End play without rehearsal, under the splenetic scrutiny of atrabilious critics.

Operation Crusader, which lasted from the middle of November, 1941, to early February, 1942, is classic as probably the most confused battle waged in Britain's military history. Vile weather and great fluidity of movement made identifying own and enemy forces as difficult as blind man's buff, from the air or on the ground. The main players in the game were to be the light and medium bombers. In the unpredicted circumstances, the calls made on them were negligible. The time between requests for air support and execution of the required response was about three hours, as the bomber airstrips were so far behind the British line. Hurricane fighter bombers were closer to the front and able to respond in thirty minutes. The system itself, however, was vindicated; and with the entry of Kittyhawks as both air superiority and bombing fighters, in March, the RAF was always superior to the enemy in performance, although outnumbered.

In November, 1942, when the Allies landed in Algeria, a new type of aircraft entered what would now be called by newspaper and television journalists, fatuously and with total ignorance of the word's meaning, the equation – when in fact 'scene' is meant. The Army now had its own artillery spotting squadrons, known as air observation posts, equipped with Auster aeroplanes flown by Royal Artillery officer pilots. Generally called AOP, their pilots referred to them as Air OP, to stress their function. This was a matter of pride and an amusing instance of that now lamentably defunct ideology of good and bad form, being an insider or an outsider, of knowing what initials such as IZ, stood for or who 'The Authentics' were. The little unarmed Auster cruised at 110 mph and would seem to have been an easy victim for German fighters. In fact, although highly dangerous to fly in the teeth of light flak or machine guns, it was so nimble that it could gleefully out-turn a Me109 or FW190 – provided the pilot saw the enemy aircraft before it came within cannon or machine-gun range. It was not uncommon for them to be blown to bits by their own artillery through flying in the path of a shell's trajectory. The Air OP squadrons did a dangerous job excellently and won not a few DFCs.

By the time the Allies landed in Italy in September, 1943, army/air co-operation had greatly improved. After years of desert warfare it had now to adapt itself to mountain country. The Rover system emerged. A Forward control unit (FCU) comprised a RAF controller, originally Group Captain David Heysham himself, hence the code name and callsign Rover David; an Army liaison officer; two R/T operators, one RAF one Army; and a RAF radio mechanic. At first they travelled in an armoured car, then a tank was tried and finally they found that a lorry with a jeep and trailer were the most efficient. The fighter bomber squadrons provided four aircraft to orbit a given point close behind the front line. These were provided in turn by the wings on orders from DAF's No 1 Mobile Operations Room Unit.

When the Army called for an attack and gave the position of the target, the Rover Controller would brief the fighter leader. Pilots and controllers had large-scale maps divided into rectangles 400 metres by 500 metres, numbered from south to north and lettered from west to east. During the Battle of Cassino these were supplemented by aerial photographs with the grid superimposed. The pilot acknowledged each item of information and the briefing began with a map reference, say, 'Target in Square C2'. Then would come a description of the relevant features of the terrain and the exact position of the target. 'Road north-east to south-west. – A third of the way down from the north-east end there is a derelict farm. – The enemy is there, with anti-tank guns in the farmhouse and the buildings on either side.' The leader might make a short dive over the target to assess it. If not, he would enlarge on the briefing when the section had it in sight, then give precise attack instructions. If the Rover unit had no targets to offer, the pilots would attack another that they had been given before take-off as an alternative. Cab ranks could be kept going all day, each flight being relieved after a fixed time.

The RAF taught the USAAF how to work with Rover Control and cab ranks, and soon 'Rover Joe' was on the air, providing close support for the 5th Army.

All the knowledge gained in the provision and control of close support was the deciding factor in ultimate victory when the air and land forces stormed the Normandy shore.

Initially, in Normandy, fighters were controlled from ships. Each of the five beaches had its own Air Staff aboard a Headquarters Ship, under whose orders there was a Fighter Direction Tender. Dusk on D-Day found 83 Group Control ashore and starting to take over from its FDT. The USAAF Control Centre was also in business. Coningham praised them both in a despatch, in which he said that they formed effective parts of a single machine, thanks to excellent teamwork between their commanders.

When the first rush was over, additions were made to the control apparatus. Armour was given its own RAF controllers, who travelled with a wireless operator in tanks whose armament had been replaced by wireless sets. Half-track contact cars were used as forward visual control posts. The Air OP pilots were so accurate in directing counter-battery fire on enemy artillery that the mere sight of an Auster was soon to become cause for the

Germans to stop shooting immediately. Where Austers could not go without the virtual certainty of being shot down, Mustangs took over. Instead of finger fours they reverted to threes, but widely spaced enough to permit them to weave while they dived and zoomed to spoil the aim of the 88s. In spite of these evasive tactics they suffered frequent casualties.

So troublesome were the enemy cannon that the Royal Artillery was given its own Rover Controller, Rover Frank, so that it could most effectively summon air support. The Army Air Support Control received the locations of enemy artillery daily from Army Group Royal Artillery. Aircraft ordered to attack confirmed their targets with their Rover Controller, who could tell them whether the sights were still active. If not, he gave them another. After an attack, pilots reported the results to him.

Air reconnaissance was as important as any of the forms of direct attack, and as vulnerable to flak and interception by Me109s and FW190s. Its organization was, like that of close air support, the beneficiary of experience gained in North Africa and Italy and as closely integrated with the relevant Army units. Tactical reconnaissance was both visual and photographic and covered an area from the enemy's forward troops to fifty miles in their rear. The requirements were: 1. A system by which the Army could request information. 2. Briefing of pilots. 3. Interrogation of pilots after the sortie. 4. The passing on of the reports. 5. Recording the results. 6. A special procedure for a direct link between ground forces in action and reconnaissance aircraft.

The depth of the area covered and the manner in which forward contact was kept varied during the campaign. The following explains the organization during the first three months.

The two most senior formations were HQ 2nd TAF and HQ 21 Army Group, which were in close liaison.

Next down the line were HQ 83 Group RAF and HQ 2nd British Army, adjacent to each other. HQ 83 Group gave instructions to No 3 (Reconnaissance) Wing, which passed them on to the airfield, where there were three low level and one high level Spitfire photographic reconnaissance squadrons.

After a sortie, the pilot was de-briefed, photographs were developed and printed, and the information obtained was transmitted from 39 Wing to 63 Group and on to HQ 2nd TAF.

HQ 84 (Reconnaissance) Group and HQ 1st Canadian Army also worked together. They had 35 Wing's two low level and one high level Spitfire squadrons at their disposal. The method of working up and down the chain of command and communication was the same.

Pilots on a sortie could make flash reports by radio, which were heard by the Group Control Centre and the airfield Operations Room. The Operations Controller could then decide whether the target reported warranted a strike. If so, he might ask the tactical reconnaissance pilot to orbit the target and transmit so that the mobile direction-finding stations could obtain a fix. The controller would then direct fighter bombers to it.

The minimum requirements to justify a strike were: 1. One or more tank(s). 2. At least ten motor vehicles. 3. At least 100 troops. 4. At least four guns. 5. All locomotives. 6. All ferries. 7. Ships over 500 tons.

The flash report gave: the map reference, a description of the target, direction of movement, any other relevant details.

In addition to the Rover Control units, there were Contact Car units. These used jeeps for suitable terrain and armoured half-tracks or tanks when necessary. The vehicles carried two R/T sets and a crew comprising a reconnaissance or fighter bomber pilot, an Air Liaison Officer (Army) and a RAF radio mechanic. They worked alongside the HQ of the leading battalion or brigade in battle, with the task of obtaining information about the ground immediately ahead of the attack. They could also do the work done by Rover Controllers if none of these was available.

All the reconnaissance systems were designed to obtain information about the immediate situation and pass it on as fast as possible.

Flight Lieutenant Geoffrey Watterson was a pilot, assessed 'Above the average', in No 4 Squadron, based at Gatwick. After the invasion the squadron continued to operate over France and he flew several reconnaissances of between fifty minutes and two hours ten minutes duration. From 8 to 10 August he was detached to airfield B10 and on 16 August the squadron moved to B4 as part of No 35 Wing. The front line was so close that some of the sorties he made when based in Normandy lasted only thirty-five minutes.

22

EVOLUTION OF AIR FORCE CLOSE SUPPORT FOR GROUND FORCES

Air support for the ground force began in 1878 when the Royal Engineers formed a balloon unit to do reconnaissance. When an expeditionary force went to Bechuanaland in 1894 it included a balloon section. The next step was the airship: the British Army acquired its first in 1907 – still for reconnaissance. In 1911 the Air Battalion of the Royal Engineers was created, comprising an airship company and an aeroplane company. The Royal Flying Corps was formed in the following year to reconnoitre and direct artillery fire.

There was contemporary development of military aviation in France, Germany, Italy and the USA. In Britain aeroplanes were accepted as more useful than airships for artillery spotting as well as reconnaissance. The first to use aircraft aggressively were the Italians, in 1912, during their war against the Turks in Libya, when they dropped bombs from an aeroplane.

During the First World War the function of aeroplanes extended to include air combat between fighters, the bombing of targets in Germany by British and French aeroplanes based in France, the escort of bombers by fighters and, eventually, ground strafing.

The emergence of the air arm from its comparatively passive to actively offensive role is largely attributable to the French. Georges Huisman, in *Dans les Coulisses de l'Aviation, 1914–1918* – Behind the Scenes of Aviation 1914–1918 – wrote, 'In August, 1914, aviation was not an arm, but a sport, at least in the minds of Army commanders. The Commander-in-Chief was a Sapper, the majority of his Staff were artillerymen: the more seriously they took dirigibles, the more they refused to regard aeroplanes as other than playthings at air shows, piloted by infantrymen and the cavalry. Some Staff College graduates who had flown on manoeuvres as observers tried to dissipate these prejudices. They did not succeed, mere lieutenants or captains, in modifying the opinion of colonels and generals. The twenty-four squadrons in service at the beginning of the war were nothing more [to the General Staff] than a means of liaison between airships and the cavalry. It was thought chimerical to expect more of them.'

In a paper entitled *Aperçus sur la Doctrine d'Emploi de l'Aéronautique Militaire Française (1914–1918)* – Summary of the Doctrine Concerning the Use of the French Military Air Arm (1914–1918) – presented to a conference at Stuttgart in 1985, a note signed by General Joffre on 10 November, 1914, is quoted: 'The air arm is not only, as has been supposed hitherto, an instrument for reconnaissance. It has rendered an extremely useful, if not indispensable, means of directing artillery fire. Further, it has shown that, by launching high explosive projectiles, it is suitable to act as an offensive arm, be it for long-range missions or in conjunction with other troops. Finally, it can pursue and destroy enemy aeroplanes.'

Joffre's conclusions were based on the performance of *l'Aviation Militaire* during the first three months of the war, which had impressed him by its contribution to victory in the first great battle, the Marne, by reconnaissance and artillery spotting. It had also revealed the eastwards movement of the enemy and had directed the guns that had been able to destroy half those of a German corps.

In the present context, it is the last three words of the penultimate sentence in his note that are most important. Here, for the first time, is mention of battlefield air support. Disappointingly, the Commander-in-Chief merely drew conclusions and stated a fact in underlining the necessity to organize the air arm according to its functions. He recommended the specialization of squadrons in three categories: reconnaissance and bombardment for those 'in the bosom of the Army' and the hunting of enemy aircraft by squadrons equipped with aeroplanes that were armoured and armed.

Joffre had already confirmed his position when, on 25 September, 1914, he appointed *Commandant* Barès to his Staff as Director of the Military Air Service. This was an officer described as 'the very soul of a flyer', the only senior one in the French Army who had flown before the war. He had, in fact, volunteered to serve as a pilot during the Balkan Wars of 1912–1913. Huisman credits him with being the inspiration for the C-in-C's note of 10 November. A few days earlier, Barès had written, 'The air arm is clearly an offensive one, in pursuit of enemy aeroplanes or destruction of troops, barracks and fortifications with bombs. It can take on specific missions at long or short range . . .'. Then comes the very first foreshadowing of a tactical air force:. . . 'or attack in conjunction with other troops'.

A Colonel Pont, commenting on Barès's paper, endorsed the principle of tactical air warfare. He expressed the general view that the air force was well suited to its present work and no more, in a narrow combat zone, but, 'It is to be hoped that in the spring we shall have squadrons with a long radius of action that can destroy or block trains and railway tracks at 200 to 250 kilometres behind the enemy lines.' At the time this passed for strategic thinking but was, in fact, tactical. The Staff remained hostile to the air arm and treated it with mistrust.

The war in the sky progressed. New aeroplanes, weapons and bombing techniques evolved, leaving the unimaginative and unenterprising to wallow in their inertia. And so we come to the dogma of mastery of the air. This ideal is unattainable, because it is expressed as an absolute, a counsel of perfection, but when modified to air superiority it becomes sustainable; and here it is in those words for the first time, in a GHQ document dated 18 January, 1916. Hitherto, the fighter opposition to the German Military Air Service had been directed by ad hoc squadron commanders, not on defined tactical principles. The Commander-in-Chief's new document dealt with the organization needed to 'sweep the enemy squadrons out of the sky'. The Germans were sending over the biggest formations of fighters yet seen. Joffre recognized the necessity to regroup the French fighter squadrons 'according to the necessities of the moment, in order to achieve an incontestable air superiority in the zones under attack'.

The enemy had the same objective – to take out the reconnaissance and artillery spotting aircraft, thus obtaining air superiority by rendering the defenders blind. The crunch came with the Battle of Verdun, which began in February, 1916. A mass of 270 German fighters attacked and succeeded in its purpose. Barèss, now a lieutenant-colonel, appointed the *Chef d'Aviation* of the 2nd Army, *Commandant* Tricornot de Rose, the first member of the French Army to qualify as a pilot, to command the squadrons defending the Verdun sector. He also increased the number of *escadrilles* in this force from four to sixteen, of which six, instead of one, were to be fighters. He put up the strength of each *escadrille* to twelve. De Rose's first innovation was to order that his fighters must operate in threes or sixes. By maintaining constant fighter patrols along the front, freedom of action for the reconnaissance and spotting aeroplanes of the 2nd Army was obtained.

This innovation turned out to be an ideological bedlam. It worked, but, for the most crass of reasons, was revoked on 17 March. The 2nd Army's Air Force Commander dispersed the six fighter squadrons among other sectors on the Verdun front on the grounds that 'it was impossible to ensure permanent patrolling of sector, because the patrols were flown on a narrrow front that limited their efficacy. The impossibility of complete coordination between neighbouring sectors meant that the patrols often occurred at the same time, while at other times the sky remained empty'. Presumably poor communications were the cause, in an era of field telephones, whose lines were short and easily cut, and wireless whose Morse transmissions were constantly distorted by atmospherics. Nonetheless, any commander incapable of regulating a timetable by some means should have been put to the customary junior pilots' chore of washing aeroplanes, not running a small air force.

This experience demonstrated that the entire force should be placed under a commander directly responsible to an Army – in this instance, the Second. It also showed that fighters should not be restricted to too defensive a role. The Commanding Officer of the already distinguished *Cigognes, Capitaine* Félix Brocard, defined the task of his new command. 'The role, of fighters is to ensure virtually constant air superiority by their permanent circulation in sufficient numbers to protect photographic [reconnaissance] and gun ranging aircraft; and offensive sorties in very great strength behind enemy lines, seeking combat'. Besides its practical worth, this officer judged such a plan for handling fighters to be of the highest psychological value to ground troops: 'The troops follow with extreme attention and lively pride the manoeuvres of aeroplanes above their heads: their aggressive attitude, their offensive incursions into enemy territory have a happy influence on morale.'

The Battle of Verdun was an essential stage in the determination of the doctrine about the use of air power. Henceforth the terms 'mastership of the air' and 'air superiority' were in frequent use. On 11 April, 1917, de Peuty, who had succeeded Barès the preceding month, issued a directive that said: 'From 15 April, fighters will resume without restriction their tactical offensive of which the purpose is the destruction of the *boche* air arm. No fighter must be met behind French lines.' He did not foresee the consequence: enemy fighters, refusing combat over their own territory, profited by the absence of opposition over the French front, assaulted it in large numbers and 'dominated the sky'. On General Nivelle's orders this was revised on 10 May. Fighters would now operate in close conjunction with the ground force.

In August, 1917, Colonel, later General, Duval took command of the air force. The Commander-in-Chief, General Pétain, wrote to the Minister for War: 'The air force has taken a leading importance: it has become one of the factors indispensable for success'. In April, 1917, the USA entered the war. In December Pétain wrote to its C-in-C, General Pershing, 'The air force will be the decisive arm if it succeeds in paralysing, during a given time and to a large extent, traffic on the enemy's lines of communication'. Desert Air Force proved the truth of this in Italy in 1944 and 2nd TAF in Normandy the same year.

The Germans had come sooner to the same conclusions without the intellectual agonizing of the French in their tortuous and torturous pursuit of logic before committing themselves to a decision. Where the Frenchman trod delicately, the *boche* clumped heavily. In Paris orders were given, then counter-manded a few weeks later. In Berlin orders were inflexible.

The concept of ground attack was obvious and the Germans produced their first purpose designed aeroplanes in 1917. The Hannover CL IIIa was a two-seater. The pilot had a forward-firing Spandau machine gun and, mounted aft of the rear cockpit so that the observer could strafe while his pilot flew low over the trenches, there was a Parabellum. The Junkers J I of the same year was all-metal and carried two Spandaus fired by the pilot and a Parabellum for the observer. The Halberstadt CL II, which came into service in 1918, was highly manoeuvrable and able to dodge ground fire, and further protected by an armour-plated belly. Pilot and observer each had a Spandau. Also introduced in 1918, the Junkers J I was another all-metal aeroplane. It had a 5mm armoured shell around the engine and was heavily armed. For the pilot, two Spandaus were housed under the engine and for the observer there was a ring-mounted Parabellum. In some the observer also had two downward-firing Parabellums.

The British were the first to add ground strafing to their repertoire. The Royal Flying Corps approached this in typically breezy fashion: pilots returning from sorties that had yielded no combat could not resist diving when they crossed the enemy front line on their way back to base and giving the trenches a good hosing, whatever type of aeroplane they were flying. There were no specially built ground attack machines. One type that was relegated to ground attack and escort duties, the de Havilland DH5, had been designed as a standard fighter. It was found to be aerodynamically inefficient, hence its limited func-tion – for which it had only a single Vickers machine gun. In

1918 the Sopwith TF2 Salamander, also a single-seater but armed with 2 Vickers machine guns and four 25lb Cooper bombs, was a late comer that did not see much service.

As early as 1916 the diary of a captured German revealed the efficacy of ground attack. 'During the day one hardly dares to be seen in the trench owing to the English aeroplanes. They fly so low that it is a wonder they do not pull one out of the trench. Nothing is to be seen of our heroic German airmen. One can hardly calculate how much additional loss of life and strain on the nerves this costs.'

One German officer admitted, 'The infantry had no training in defence against very low-flying aircraft. Moreover, they had no confidence in their ability to shoot these machines down if they were determined to press home their attacks. As a result, they were seized with a fear amounting almost to panic; a fear that was fostered by the incessant activity and hostility of enemy aeroplanes.'

A German private writing home complained, 'We are in reserve but cannot remain long on account of hostile aircraft. About our own aeroplanes one must be almost too ashamed to write. It is simply scandalous. They fly as far as this village but no further, whereas the English are always flying over our lines.'

The French never did get around to designing an aeroplane specifically for ground strafing. While they were analysing the theory of tactical air support and thinking in terms of bombers, they were sending fighters across the enemy lines. These could have used the opportunity to terrify the German infantry in their trenches. The Germans were waiting until they were equipped with specialist and well protected aeroplanes before they set about strafing. The British gave it a try, found that their aircraft were adequate and the results worthwhile, so carried on as a matter of course. By 1918, this demanded considerable guts – trench strafing had become so risky that it was the most hated of all duties. Machine gun and concerted rifle fire from the front and support trenches was severe, hugging the ground meant having to fly very low without crashing at the same time as firing the gun; when several machines were attacking, collision risk was high, especially when breaking after a run.

Since 1916 the British had also been giving the infantry tactical air support, although without calling it by that name. It was not in the form of ground strafing but of reporting by wireless the forward positions of infantry in attack. The soldiers tried various means of identifying themselves to pilots and observers: metal panels on their back packs to reflect sunlight, or yellow patches that showed through the smoke and gloom, large strips of white cloth that not only showed where they were but also their regiment, and Verey lights.

Britain made more progress in air support than any other country, and should have developed it further than it did by the time of the Second World War. After the First World War the RAF had a unique function that gave it the opportunity to practise close support, particularly light armoured vehicles – one of the many benefits of empire. When, in 1919, Mesopotamia became the new Kingdom of Iraq and was under British mandate, Britain was faced with an unprecedented task: to exercise effective military control over thousands of square miles of desert in which lay scattered villages and encampments to keep under surveillance as well as warlike nomadic tribes who often fought each other. The only way to do this was from the air, so the RAF was, for the first time in history, appointed to be in command of all military operations. There was a British infantry regiment in Iraq and native levies, commanded by British officers, were also recruited. The RAF formed its own armoured car squadrons. Air, armoured vehicles and infantry worked closely together.

The Arabs were also a danger to RAF crews: not only those who had to make forced landings through engine trouble, but also anyone flying low, who presented a tempting target for rifle practice. The best known British airman who pioneered long distance flights in the early 1920s was Sir Alan Cobham, a wartime pilot. In 1926, when making the first return flight from England to Australia, a sandstorm between Baghdad and Basra forced him to fly low. A bullet fired from the ground hit his mechanic, Elliott and wounded him so badly that he died a few hours later.

On the north-west frontier of India, the British and Indian Armies had been keeping the peace since the mid-19th Century. Tribesmen from Afghanistan waged an unceasing guerilla war against them. From 1919 RAF squadrons were stationed in the area to give the infantry and mountain artillery close support.

Despite the advantages of such diverse training under campaign conditions, combined operations languished. The air side dwindled into a few army co-operation squadrons in which no RAF pilots were keen to serve, because it was boring.

The outbreak of war in 1939 found Britain poorly placed to cope with such a breathtaking innovation as the *Blitzkrieg*. After the defeat of the French and British forces in France in June, 1940, the British Army immediately introduced two vital innovations – the Commandos and the Parachute Regiment. The opportunity to devise an even more necessary modernisation, close air support, without which the other two could not function to their full potential, arose at the same time. The missing link that had to be forged was close liaison between and efficient joint operations by, the three Services – particularly air and ground. The need to do so was hastened by the start of the second foreign campaign of the war, which began on 10 June, 1940, when Italy declared war against Britain and became Germany's ally. The Royal Air Force, Royal Navy and British Army stationed in Egypt were immediately in arms against an Italian and colonial Army in neighbouring Libya that numbered 300,000 and an air force of 282 aeroplanes. There were only 36,000 British, Indian and New Zealand troops in Egypt, and 165 RAF aircraft. The RAF made its first attack on the Italians at dawn on 11 June, the Army made a foray across the Libyan frontier on the 12th and the Navy carried out a sweep against Tobruk on the same day.

The instant creation of an imperative support for the Army in all its operations against the enemy and for the Navy in many of theirs, was the catalyst that converted stagnation into creative activity.

By the Normandy D-Day the RAF had evolved a system of battlefield air support that was as near perfection as was attainable with the means then available.

INDEX

with last German fighter shot down by Typhoons, 137.

Galland, Lieutenant-General Adolf, Luftwaffe Commander of Fighters: describes plight of Luftwaffe under heavy air attack by RAF and USAAF, 73; describes how German High Command was taken by surprise and criticises its ineptitudes, 86–92; friendship with Wing Commander J. E. J. Johnson, 127; describes Luftwaffe fighters' operating conditions in July and August, 128–129.

Geerte, Squadron Leader Manu, DFC, 57

Gillam, Group Captain D. E., DSO and two bars, DFC and bar, leads Typhoon attack on Gestapo headquarters in Amsterdam, 132; method of attack with cannon and machine guns, 143.

Gold Beach, air fighting over on D-Day, 49

Great Massingham, Norfolk; base of 169 Sqdn, 29.

Giscion, Colonel Jean, 72

Green, Wing Commander DFC, CO 121 Wing, 67

Green, Flight Sergeant: shot down, killed, 133

Group Control Centre, 156

Hamilton, Flying Officer, 132.

Harwell, Berkshire, Base of 295 Sqdn, 22, 23.

Hasson, Sergeant, Boissieux's air gunner, 57.

Hilgendorf, *Oberleutnant* Viktor, one-legged and oldest pilot in JG26, 94–95.

Hulme, Sergeant Bill. Kingdon's air gunner, 25.

Hunt, Corporal F. R., 111.

Ingham, Leading Aircraftman Eric: crosses to Normandy in FDT216 on night 5/6 June; experiences in Operations room; ship torpedoed, 44–46.

Jeffries, Flight Lieutenant, 53-year-old Hurricane and B17 pilot, 11

Johnson, Wing Commander J. E. J. (later Air Vice Marshal, CB, CBE, DSO and two bars, DFC). Commanding 144 (Spitfire) Wing of three Canadian squadrons 441, 443, 40–41, 144; Wing lands and refuels at airstrip B3, 74, 75; friendship with Galland, 127; method of dive-bombing, 139.

Juno Beach. Air activity on D-Day, 53.

Kemmis, Flying Officer P. Woodman's observer, 29.

Kingaby, Wing Commander, DFM and two bars, 58; praises 345 Sqdn, 106.

Kingdon, Flight Lieutenant Oliver, Albemarle pilot, 295 Sqdn, Harwell, Berks, 23–25.

Knoke, Hauptmann Heinz, fighter Staffel Commander; describes squadron life and his air battles, 96–102.

Lallement, Squadron Leader Raymond DFC and bar, ('Cheval'), 57; method of rocket attack, 141.

Layton, Flying Officer, navigator to Bulloch: wins DSO, 6.

Lee, Flight Lieutenant R., DFC, shot

down, his Typhoon overturns, on top of him and he is rescued a week later, 120.

Losses, Allied by D plus 7, 74.

Luftwaffe, Fighter and Bomber strength in Northern France, Belgium and Holland on D-Day, 41; Torpedo bombers operating off beachheads and over Channel; 76–85; losses at D plus 31, 74: order of battle, 88; sorties flown on 30 June, 108; technical officer describes operating conditions July and August, 128, 129.

Mallard, Operation, parachute drop by Albemarles on 6 June, 23–25.

Maquis, French Resistance organization, 35–38.

Martell, Christian, on D-Day, 53.

Matthews, Flight Sergeant (later Warrant Officer), Cleaver's navigator bales out and joins Maquis, 38

McQuarrie, Ed, RCAF, Bulmer's navigator in 21 Sqdn (Mosquitoes, 47.

McQuillin, Aircraftman Alan, 62.

Minesweepers attacked by Typhoons, 124–126.

Merriman, Corporal Geoffrey, MBE, 111

Morgan, Pilot Officer David. In fight with last German fighter shot down by Typhoons, 137.

Muddiman, Sergeant Alan, Archer's navigator, 24–25.

Mulberry, artificial harbour, 14.

Offenberg, Flight Lieutenant Jean, First Belgian awarded DFC, 57.

Oldest Squadron Commander in history, 12.

Ouistreham, 23, 24.

Peaslee, Colonel Budd, USAAF. Forms First Scouting Force to fly weather reconnaissance in Mustangs ahead of day bombers, 10.

Priller, *Oberstleutnant* Josef ('Pips'), *Kommodore* JG26(Schlageter). His 99th and 100th victories, 92–94.

Radar, Number of radar stations on French coast and Allied counter-measures prior to D-Day, 14; counter-measure Mosquitoes, 28–29: on board FDT216, 43, 44.

Radar and Mobile Signals Units (RAMSU): description of Rebecca-Eureka equipment, 109, RAMSU lands in Normandy, 111; under shellfire, 112.

RAF Regiment, 103.

Ramage, Sergeant W. R., 2 i/c paratroop stick dropped on night 5/6 June, 25–28.

Resistance Organization, French, 35–38.

Read, Leading Aircraftman: joins FDT 216, crosses to Normandy on night 5/6 June and is torpedoed, 43–46.

Rommel, Field-Marshal Irwin; headquarters attacked by Typhoons, 57.

Rotterdam, Typhoons destroy Gestapo Headquarters, 132, 133.

Rover Control, 150, 153, 154, 155.